MEDITATIONS ON
ACCORDING TO JOHN

EXERCISES IN BIBLICAL THEOLOGY

HEROLD WEISS

Energion Publications
Gonzalez, FL
2014

Copyright © 2014, Herold Weiss

Unless otherwise noted, Scripture quotations are from the Revised Standard Version of the Bible, copyright © 1946, 1952, and 1971 National Council of the Churches of Christ in the United States of America. Used by permission. All rights reserved.

Cover Design: Henry E. Neufeld

Cover Image Credits:
Nail Pierced Feet: 16672667 © Federicofoto | Dreamstime.com
Foot Washing: 6873941 © Jozef Sedmak | Dreamstime.com

ISBN10: 1-63199-012-8
ISBN13: 978-1-63199-012-0
Library of Congress Control Number: 2014909400

Energion Publications
P. O. Box 841
Gonzalez, FL 32560

energion.com
pubs@energion.com
850-525-3916

PRAISE FOR *MEDITATIONS ON ACCORDING TO JOHN*

Dr. Herold Weiss' meditations on the Gospel of John will surprise no one familiar with his other valuable contributions to our understanding of the message of Scripture and of Christian faith. As he has throughout a half century of scholarship, teaching, preaching and writing, he here brings to focus his richly informed familiarity with the best in contemporary scholarship on the New Testament and his gifted sensitivity to the spiritual intent of the Fourth Gospel. His book will open the eyes of many to new riches in this Gospel.

Earle Hilgert, Professor of New Testament, emeritus
McCormick Theological Seminary

Meditations on According to John draws readers enticingly into the theological world of John's Gospel. Herold Weiss, a gifted guide, explores this world through the lens of theological and devotional reflection, which Weiss finds rooted in the traditional understanding of "meditations" on the Scriptures. Although engagingly brief, each chapter contains rich insights into key phrases from the gospel which serve as his chapter titles. Weiss shows how a phrase in one part of the gospel illuminates theological concepts that are crucial to the whole work. The interdisciplinary nature of Weiss' approach enhances the theological insights by placing them in their philosophical and cultural milieu as well as within their literary context. Fascinated by the ways *According to John* gives readers a window into the faith of particular Christian communities living at the end of the first century, Weiss helps contemporary readers listen more carefully to the nuances and unique contributions of that faith. His meditations, like the gospel stories and discourses themselves, invite re-readings. Familiar stories become new again, calling for further meditation. I look forward to reading this book with my students, challenged to embrace the life of the "realm above" that shaped the faith of the Johannine community.

Kendra Haloviak Valentine
Associate Professor of Biblical Studies, La Sierra University

When Weiss walks you through the Gospel of John, the maze turns to amazement. You will discover another world with all the favorable conditions for a better life.

Abraham Terian, Professor of Early Christianity and Dean, emeritus, St. Nersess Armenian Seminary

Just as Philip invites Nathaniel to consider who Jesus is in the Gospel of John by saying "come and see," Herold Weiss invites readers to do likewise by engaging important passages from that gospel. Weiss' "meditations" are exegetical reflections on the fourth gospel that convey his learning, insights, and interests that have been developed over a long career studying the sacred writings of ancient Israel and early Christianity in their historical contexts. In this way, *Meditations on According to John* offers fruits of historical-critical study on the fourth gospel to non-specialists without unnecessary scholarly jargon, while simultaneously proposing fresh interpretations for today. Weiss's book is a welcome contribution to all those interested in "meditating" on the fourth gospel and on its presentation of Jesus.

John Fotopoulos, Associate Professor of Religious Studies Saint Mary's College, Notre Dame, IN

Weiss is the perfect guide into the world of this notoriously difficult gospel, and the book's structure—a series of meditations on its theology—turns out to be a rich and rewarding way to enter into it, if not ideal. Weiss walks the reader through the complex symbolic world of the fourth gospel, carefully revealing some of the sometimes surprising threads that run through it and at the same time situating the text within the larger contexts of emerging early Christianity, Judaism, and the larger Greco-Roman world. Weiss has a knack for unpacking and explaining the complex philosophical ideas and cultural backgrounds that prove essential to making sense of this gospel.

Ruben Dupertuis, Associate Professor of Religion Trinity University, San Antonio, TX

Dedicated to the memory of

"la Mutter"

Julia Weiss Riffel
(1880 – 1963)

Table of Contents

Preface vii
Introduction 1
1 In the Beginning Was the Logos 15
2 Making Himself Equal with God 21
3 He Who Follows Me … Will Have the Light of Life 29
4 No One Has Ascended into Heaven 35
5 Of His Fullness We Have All Received 43
6 To Bear Witness to the Truth 51
7 Who Is this Son of Man? 59
8 The Hour Is Coming, and Now Is 69
9 On the Third Day 77
10 I Finished the Work 85
11 The Law Was Given through Moses 93
12 I Have Overcome the World 101
13 It Is Not by Measure that God Gives the Spirit 109
14 Remember My Words 117
15 Salvation Is from the Jews 125
16 Did I Not Choose You, the Twelve? 133
17 The House was Filled
      with the Fragrance of Her Ointment 143
18 Clean by the Word 151
19 We Must Work While It Is Day 159
20 United by Love 167
21 Jesus Wept 177
22 Rivers of Living Water 187
23 Where Are You From? 195
24 Abide in my Love 205
    Epilogue 211

Preface

This book is the realization of a long-held dream. During my first semester as a doctoral student, in 1958, I discovered the depths to which the language of *According to John* invites its readers. Since then my admiration for this gospel grew as I spent time exploring its many large chambers of meaning below its surface in preparation for teaching. In this endeavor, of course, I was helped by other scholars who had already devoted concerted efforts to understand its message. It may not be an exaggeration to say that no other New Testament book has received as much attention and as a result has been so drastically re-interpreted during the last fifty years or so.

Many times I had the feeling that I should try to write a book that put these advances in our knowledge within reach of a larger audience. The treasures in the gospel should not be confined to the scholarly community. What prevented me from writing the book was my inability to decide on the format into which to put its insights. Then in 2009 I was invited to write a monthly column at www.spectrummagazine.com. The editors of this web page graciously gave me total freedom on choosing the subjects of my columns. It did not take long for me to realize that deciding on the subject of a column was half the task. This led me to write series of columns on a subject, thus limiting the horizon within which to search for the subject of the next column. My second series dealt with the gospel *According to John*. Thus, without long-term planning and under the pressure of a monthly deadline, I began writing columns on aspects of this gospel. In the process I discovered that they were the format I had been searching for. The original columns, re-written, expanded, re-organized and polished without the pressure of deadlines, now appear as meditations for the benefit of a different audience. My hope is that their readers will experience as great a sense of fulfillment as I have had in writing them.

I have named these exercises in biblical theology "meditations" to underline their purpose. These days a meditation is understood to be a help for devotions. Meditations, however, have a long tradition as philosophical reflections. It goes back to the first translators of the Roman emperor Marcus Aurelius' "Meditations." Marcus titled his philosophical musings "To Himself," *Eis heauton* in Greek. His meditations are not just a loose collection of observations or insights that one wishes to save for future reference. They are a philosophy of life with a central guiding principle considered worthy of the attention of others. My meditations on *According to John* are intended to be both theological musings and devotional helps. They were written as explorations of a way of life and its symbolic universe to open a window for the benefit of others.

I have always considered writing to be an activity that while carried out in private is done in dialogue with others. This is true both in the actual writing of the first drafts, when one's interlocutors are in one's imagination, and in the actual back and forth with those with whom one shares drafts in order to receive comments, criticisms or suggestions. The final draft of this book owes much to three friends who gave me most valuable feedback. Terence Martin, a long time colleague and friend from my years teaching at Saint Mary's College, Notre Dame, read the full text and gave me much support and advice at leisurely, lively lunches. Jean and Don Rhoads, long-standing friends since the time when Don and I were beginning our academic careers, read these pages with much care and offered most acute comments about their content. To these friends I owe a great debt of gratitude. As always, Henry Neufeld, my editor and publisher, distinguished himself by his enthusiasm for the project and his professional competence. As the one actually making the book available to the reading public, he has my most sincere admiration. The book is dedicated to "la Mutter," my grandmother, a woman with an indomitable spirit, a generous heart and an intuitive desire to serve. She helped women give birth to countless babies in a forgotten countryside in Argentina. Her life was a testimony to the value of both the fleshly and the spiritual birth.

Introduction

From a strictly historical point of view, one of the details of the life of Jesus about which there is absolute agreement is that he was crucified by the Roman procurator Pontius Pilate. It is also quite certain that at the crucifixion Jesus' disciples thought that their investment in Jesus had become a losing proposition. They decided, therefore, to return to the fishing business, as the last chapter of *According to John* reports. The announcements that Jesus was alive and had been seen by responsible disciples took them by surprise. This new fact was understood among early followers of the Jesus Movement in two quite different ways.

Those followers of Jesus who harbored apocalyptic expectations immediately understood that God had raised Jesus from the dead. This gave them a totally different understanding of what had been going on during the time they had spent with Jesus, as well as a new meaning to the crucifixion. Until then they thought they had witnessed an execution. Now they had to re-interpret its purpose. We do not know how they made sense at first of what they had experienced. There is a gap of about twenty years between the death of Jesus and the ministry of Paul, the first Christian whose writings we possess. He placed the crucifixion and the resurrection in a dramatic and unique apocalyptic cosmic horizon. According to him, Jesus' death had been the triumph of God over the power of sin and death. It meant that human life, which since the sin of Adam had been in a world under evil powers, is no longer unavoidably under their dominion. On the one hand, the death of Jesus put an end to the stranglehold these powers had over all human beings. On the other hand, by the resurrection of Christ, God carried out a New Creation by the power of the Spirit. In other words, the world that resulted from the Fall of Adam had come to an end. The Risen Christ is the Second Adam and the first being of a new life in the Spirit. The cross and the resurrection are the pivot on which the ages turn. His death was the end of this present Evil Age, and his resurrection the inauguration of the Age of Messiah, which any day soon would culminate in the Age to Come. The apocalyptic doctrine of the two ages gave Paul the framework within which to understand what God had done at the cross and the resurrection.

Other Christians, those who did not share the apocalyptic mind set, understood that the fact that Jesus was now alive meant that he actually was a divine being who had not died on the cross. The Roman soldiers certainly crucified a body, but the divine being who had used that body during his earthly mission abandoned it once he no longer needed it. Thus, the incarnated divine being had not died on a cross. Jesus was not a human being at all. He was a divine being in a human body. His mission had been to actualize before human beings God's love for God's creatures and to communicate to them how to live a life that would become eternal in God's very abode. Jesus' presence among humans gave them a clear object on which to exercise faith and gain knowledge of God's final intentions for them. The crucifixion had been the trampoline that launched his ascent back to the Father.

Eventually Christians came to understand the Christ event in terms that incorporated elements of both initial explanations. The dominant view insisted on the reality of the incarnation of a divine being and that Jesus had actually died on the cross. The view that Jesus had been an immortal divine being who only appeared to be human was then declared anathema. It became known as docetism, the first Christian heresy. Its explicit condemnation is found in the words of John the Elder: "Every spirit that confesses that Jesus Christ has come in the flesh is of God, and every spirit which does not confess Jesus [in the flesh] is not of God" (1 John 4:2 – 3).

According to John had its origin within a Christian community that viewed Jesus as a divine manifestation of God. When Christianity made it a test of faith to affirm the reality of the incarnation into a human being who actually died and had been raised from the dead, the Johannine community joined the Christian mainstream.

Unlike the Gospel of Thomas, for example, which contains only sayings of Jesus and overlooks his death, presenting him as a divine being who imparts esoteric wisdom, *According to John* contains a narrative of his trial and crucifixion and makes explicit reference to his resurrection (20:8). Moreover, the post-resurrection appearance to Thomas is an explicit anti-docetic argument that ties the Risen Christ to the body that died on the cross.

Still, in *According to John's* account of his capture at the Garden of Gethsemane and his trial, Jesus is always in command of the situation. At the garden there is no agony, and Judas does not betray him with a kiss. Speaking of his imminent departure from this world, Jesus claims to have the power to put down his life and the power to take it up again (10:18). In the trial before Pilate the power of the Roman Empire is declared derivative (19:11). John the Baptist does not baptize him with the baptism of repentance for the forgiveness of sins (1:29 – 34). Throughout his ministry he can read what is in the minds of others without their speaking (2:24 – 25). This has caused scholars to see in this gospel a tacit or implicit docetism. That is, while the gospel in its final form is clearly anti-docetic, making the point that the Christ who appeared to the disciples after the crucifixion had the body with the marks of the nails and the spear that had pierced it at the cross, it does present a Jesus who is fully divine and may legitimately be worshipped (9:38). It would seem, therefore, that the gospel took initial shape in a community that understood the fact that Jesus was alive after his crucifixion in terms of his divine origin, quite apart from an apocalyptic framework. That picture of Jesus makes him not really human. Those elements of this picture, which eventually came to be identified as docetic, belong to the early stages in the development of the gospel, when the Johannine community was somewhat isolated from the rest of Christianity. By the time the gospel was integrated into the Christian mainstream and began to circulate together with the synoptics, it had been edited to emphasize the reality of his death.

Recognizing the diversity that characterized early Christianity is the key to an understanding of the origins and the purpose of *According to John*. Up until the middle of the twentieth century critical scholarship more or less took for granted that this gospel had been written in the second century by a Christian who wished to make Christianity understandable to a Hellenistic audience. With this in mind the author had left out the apocalyptic message of Jesus and transposed the message of Jesus into a Hellenistic key. According to this view, the gospel was the culmination of a straight line of theological development which began with the Synoptic gospels, was developed by Paul in his letters and reached its climax in *According to John*. The discovery of the Dead Sea Scrolls, however, made it clear that Judaism, and even the apocalyptic sectarian community at Qumran, was thoroughly Hellenized by Jesus' time. The then popular distinctions between Hebraic and Hellenistic thought and between Palestinian and Diaspora Judaism were severely modified by the new evidence. The old model for understanding the oral traditions about Jesus, which classified them by determining whether they came from a Jewish-Palestinian-Aramaic speaking, a Jewish-Palestinian-Greek speaking, a Jewish-Greek-speaking-Diaspora, or a Gentile-Greek speaking environment, has been thoroughly rejected. Most scholars now agree that *According to John* was not written by a disciple of Jesus on the basis of his participation in the story, or by a late author who sat down to write a gospel to attract Hellenists to Christ using oral traditions that circulated in a Gentile-Greek speaking environment.

It seems most likely that the writing now known as *According to John* took shape in a Christian community within Judaism that over time revised and added materials to its foundational document. What we have is an in-house document that served to give meaning to the significant experiences in the life of this community. The members of this community had belonged previously to Jewish groups in the periphery and did not belong to what eventually became mainstream Christianity. They developed their own way of understanding the significance of Jesus' life and an internal vocabulary with which to express it. This accounts for its highly evocative but simple language. It echoes as it bounces off the walls.

The Christians who produced this gospel were an enclosed community distinct from the main currents of the early Christian movement. Their "jargon" resonated clearly among them. To read *According to John* requires being aware that, as Louis J. Martyn explained brilliantly some forty years ago, it contains simultaneously two stories. Obviously we are reading about the life of Jesus, but at the same time we are reading about the experience of a community of Christians with a singular history. It appears that most of its members had been thrown out of a synagogue and they are having heated debates both with members of the synagogue from which they had been expelled and with other Christians who do not share their view of Jesus. While telling the story of Jesus these Christians were also explaining to themselves the meaning of what was happening to them. In other words they told the story of Jesus to understand what they were experiencing. By telling the story of Jesus they were establishing the meaning of their lives. Thus, for example, the dialogue between Jesus and Nicodemus, where Jesus speaks in the first person singular, is suddenly interrupted by the words: "we speak of what we know, and bear witness to what we have seen; but you (plural) do not receive our testimony" (3:11). This is clearly a declaration being made by the Johannine community some decades after the death of Jesus.

As Raymond E. Brown has most effectively explained, the community apparently started with former disciples of John the Baptist and other Jews from the fringes together with Samaritans. Quite likely it also counted among its members relatives of Jesus, more specifically, his mother. Its geographical location is now impossible to determine. Probably it resided in a locality where Gentile God-fearers, that is Gentiles attracted to Judaism, were numerous, and some of them also joined the group.

As a community on the fringes it had tensions with both Jewish and Christian communities. The Jewish synagogue to which most of its members had been attached decided to expel them on account of their claims of divinity for Jesus. This claim was a direct challenge to Judaism's only doctrine: God is one. Expulsion from the synagogue was a traumatic experience for these Johannine Christians. When push came to shove, some who had been attracted to Jesus, but who were anxious about retaining their social position, decided not to make their faith in Jesus public. They feared the social and economic consequences of expulsion from the synagogue (12:42 – 43) and became disciples "of the night" like Nicodemus (3:1; 7:50; 19:39), or "secret disciples" like Joseph of Arimathea (19:38).

The text now contains vitriolic arguments against the Jews who refused to believe that Jesus was the One Sent by the Father to reveal eternal life to humanity. The animosity between the Johannine and the Rabbinic communities created by the expulsion of the Christians from the synagogue produced strong charges against the Jews. In the meditations that follow I write "the Jews" with quotation marks to alert the reader that the reference is one made by a particular Christian community in the midst of a fierce struggle with Jews who toward the end of the first century had disowned them. "The Jews," much to the confusion of these Christians, had refused to believe the claims of divinity which they were making for Jesus. This portrayal of the Jews does not fit the Jews who were the contemporaries of Jesus, or Jews in general. All historical reconstructions of the life of Jesus and of his death agree that he was put to death by the Romans. The evidence also indicates that Christians continued to worship at the temple and considered themselves good Jews after the crucifixion. Unlike the apostle Paul, who considered himself a Jew and was proud of it throughout his life, the Johannine Christians eventually broke their ties to Judaism and the law. Thus, while *According to John* presupposes thorough knowledge of the Jewish Scriptures, it presents Jesus as one who is the superior alternative to the law and consigns the law to "the Jews."

It appears, then, that *According to John* was an internal document in which the members of the Johannine community interpreted their own experiences as Jews in the light of what they knew about the life of Jesus according to the oral traditions available to them. As such, the gospel is a document which aims to build up the faith of the members of a community that understands its own history in light of the story of Jesus and has adapted the traditions about Jesus to make sense of their own experience. Like the other three gospels, the fourth gospel was written anonymously. All four gospels were given identifying titles when they were collected and published together early in the second century. The ancient manuscripts and modern critical editions of the text of the New Testament name the fourth gospel as *According to John* (KATA IOANNEN). By adopting this tradition I wish to indicate the artificiality of the title. I will refer to the one who describes or explains what took place as "the narrator." As has been noted the gospel took shape over a period of about fifty years with several hands adding to and editing the story. There were, therefore, several anonymous narrators.

That the gospel functioned as an internal document of a sectarian community is evident also by the way it is written. The story of Jesus is not told so as to lead the reader step by step to an understanding of Jesus as the One Sent from heaven by the Father to bring life to humanity. Readers do not have to wait until the end of the story to receive the momentous disclosure of the significance of Jesus' mission. Instead, it is presupposed that they already know how the story ends. From the very beginning readers must have a good grasp of the symbolic universe of the gospel. They must know the different levels of meaning in which the vocabulary works. Thy must know the echo chamber within which the gospel's language resonates. This outstanding characteristic of *According to John* is clear evidence of its sociological positioning. The language is almost a dialect shared by the members of the sect.

This means that the connections between the stories which are found in both *According to John* and the Synoptic Gospels are not to be read as attempts on the part of this gospel to correct or improve the Synoptic accounts. The connection is to be seen at the level of the oral traditions that were developed along different trajectories in different Christian communities facing different circumstances. It also means that attempts to reconstruct a "historical Jesus" by harmonizing the accounts of the four gospels do not in fact reconstruct the life of Jesus with any historical accuracy. The harmonization of the gospel accounts only succeeds in creating a fifth narrative according to the predilection of people with theological views that are favored by members of a Christian community in the present.

The outline of the ministry of Jesus in the synoptic gospels was designed by *According to Mark*. It describes a rather short period spent in Galilee of the Gentiles during which Jesus distinguishes himself by his miracles and his controversies with Pharisees. During a trip to the north, at Caesarea Philippi close to the fountains of the Jordan River, Peter confesses that Jesus is the Christ (the Messiah, Mk. 8:29), and his confession causes Jesus to demand complete silence about his identity. When evil spirits that Jesus expelled from possessed people cried out that Jesus was the Son of God, Jesus also gave them strict orders to keep silent and not reveal his identity. Peter's confession marks the turning point in Jesus' ministry in the lands of the gentiles and brings about Jesus' decision to go to Jerusalem. Upon arriving at the city, immediately he finds himself opposed by the Sadducees who control the temple and have influence with the Roman procurator Pontius Pilate. Five days after coming to Jerusalem, Jesus hangs from a cross on a small hill outside the city. *According to Matthew* and *According to Luke* add to this outline narratives of Jesus' birth, of the resurrection and of post resurrection appearances which are peculiar to each of them (in the best manuscripts *According to Mark* ends in 16:8).

According to John was conceived in a different womb and differs notably from the synoptics: here Jesus' ministry includes Jerusalem from the beginning, and his final stay in the city lasts six months, from the feast of Tabernacles (September/October) till Passover (April/May). In this gospel, rather than imposing silence on those publicly identifying him, Jesus insists that he must be identified correctly, not just as Son of God, but as God. These differences cannot be overlooked, and place the gospel in a category by itself, as the early Church Fathers already recognized.

It has been argued that *According to John* consists of two sections identified as: "The Book of Signs" and the "The Book of Glory." Others have proposed that rather than dividing the text into sections one should identify the *sources* used for its composition. It has been posited, for example, that the author used a source which contained several miracles. This is supported by the numbering of the changing of water into wine (2:1 – 11) and the healing of the son of the imperial officer (4:46 – 54) as the first and the second signs. The ending of the gospel in 20:30 – 31, then, is taken to have been the ending of the Signs Source. What makes the numbering of the two signs evidence of an underlying source is that in the gospel text the cleansing of the temple appears in between them, making the healing of the Roman official's son the third sign.

Besides the Signs Source, a second source is identified as the one that provided the Revelation Discourses. These are extended monologues in which Jesus presents himself as I AM, the revealer of the Father. To these two sources ably redacted into the present text, it is argued, the authors then added the narrative of the passion, death and resurrection taken from the oral tradition.

A more recent theory identifies sources separating sections where miracles are called signs from sections in which they are called works. The problem with all these reconstructions of the origin of the gospel text in our possession, however, is that they lack a foundation that is based on broad appeals to vocabulary, style or theological perspectives. Against all source theories, it must be noted, the text displays amazing stylistic, verbal and theological integrity. Lacking sufficient supporting evidence, these various source theories have not been widely adopted. Still, many recognize that there may have been a collection of miracle stories which supplied material to the gospel.

In its present form, the gospel contains several inconsistencies or discontinuities. I have already pointed to docetic elements and an anti-docetic stand. I have also mentioned the numbering of the third sign as the second, and that at some points the narrative is interrupted by a communal confession. Some narrative sequences now appear to be dislodged, so that 7:15 – 24 clearly belongs together with the story of the healing of the paralytic at Bethesda (5:1 – 16). The text contains not only two justifications for the authority of Jesus to command the healed paralytic to carry his bed on a Sabbath, but also two rationales for the washing of the disciples' feet (13:10 – 17), and two Farewell Discourses. The Farewell Discourse which ends in 14:31 with the words "Rise, let us go hence" belongs together with the beginning of chapter 18. Chapters 15 – 17, then, seem a later addition. If the order of chapters 5 and 6 is reversed the topographical references to Jerusalem and the Sea of Galilee fit more cogently within the overall narrative. Chapter 20 has a clear ending for the gospel as a whole. The second ending in 21:24 -25 is obviously an afterthought, made necessary by the addition of chapter 21.

These many perplexing difficulties may be taken to indicate that the gospel developed over a period of time with sections added into an existing text as circumstances changed. Nearly everyone agrees that the final revision took place between 95 and 110 CE. At one time the gospel was dated between 150 and 175 CE. The discovery of a little scrap of papyrus containing words of chapter 17 on the front and words of chapter 18 on the reverse has made that dating impossible. This papyrus fragment was found in Egypt and is dated between 125 and 150 CE. The earliest full text of the gospel now in our possession is part of an Egyptian papyrus codex dated around 175 CE.

The characteristics of *According to John* which I have been describing serve to increase the desire to plumb its depths and appreciate its message. The complexity of its origin within one of the many trajectories adopted by different communities of the Jesus Movement in their attempts to understand God's workings in the person of Jesus reveals the theological creativity of those Christians and has left us with an enticing and somewhat enigmatic gospel. Attempts to understand it, therefore, must be characterized by humility. No one may claim to have established the absolutely correct interpretation of its message. The text allows for many valid interpretations. Still, anyone who intends to explore its horizon and plumb its depths has to choose what at the moment seems to be the most valid among them. Those of us reading the gospel in the twenty-first century can only struggle trying to penetrate the meaning that to the original community must have been quite plain. No one can guarantee that she or he has captured the meaning as a whole. The cultural patterns of thought in the first century are not at all ours. Faced with this barrier I have opted for describing as best I can what the text says in terms of my understanding of its symbolic universe. This does not mean that I accept as valid all its presuppositions or its points of view, or that I find its presentation of themes quite satisfactory. For example, I find quite inadequate the notion that sickness is caused by sin (9:2), and the pervasive tension between determinism and free will: only those who are drawn by God come to Jesus, but those who refuse to believe are condemned. The notion that a woman's purpose in life is primarily to bear children (16:21) is also quite problematic. Even as I find the vision of living abiding in Christ quite admirable, I would have liked for the gospel to give a more concrete picture of how such a life looks like.

Thus, while the gospel contains elements which may be foreign to us, it still offers a marvelous vision of the significance of Jesus, the man who many saw merely as the son of Joseph and Mary and others saw as the Son of God. The vision of the latter group is one that sparks a desire to understand it and to wonder about the implications it contains. Its influence in the history of Christianity, it would seem, has been enormous, well beyond the highest expectations the Johannine community may have had. Any attempt to enter that world must begin with the study of the grammar of the Johannine language, recognizing its significance and attempting to penetrate its inner resonances. The language is the carrier of the theology of the community. Theology is the result of faith being expressed within cultural parameters and a meaningful symbolic universe. The following meditations are my attempts to understand the theology of the Johannine community.

As do other books of the Bible, *According to John* reveals how some of the early Christians expressed their faith fully, creatively, powerfully within their symbolic universe and cultural parameters. The Christian Gospel, no doubt, transcends all its expressions and their cultural limitations. As such it is capable of being expressed in any culture and in any symbolic universe. Letting a text of Scripture speak for itself in its own voice causes one to marvel at the visions it projects. After all, Jesus did not come to reveal information about this or that. He came to reveal life, and he lived in full possession of it in order to give it to others.

According to John understands the Gospel as the communication of the power of life as truth itself. Both Paul and *According to John* point out that when truth and love are in tension, love is to be given precedence because God is love. To live the faith is to live life faithfully, not to live THE FAITH as an imposed dogmatic truth.

I began this introduction with the phrase "from a strictly historical point of view." My intention, however, is not to read the gospel historically in an attempt to reconstruct the life of Jesus or that of the Johannine community. I depend on the light thrown by historical research, however, to capture the theological ways in which this gospel presents Jesus and a Christian community united by bonds of love within a world that threatens its very existence. As a community that lived in the world but saw itself apart from the world, it came to appreciate a way to life in the world sustained by the Spirit that the Son had breathed on his disciples before his return to the Father (20:22). The vision of the life of faith exposed in their foundational document has been a permanent source of comfort to Christians through the centuries.

One of the purposes of this book of meditations is to demonstrate that it is quite possible to take seriously the results of modern critical study of the ancient texts and be a modern believer in the One Sent by the Father. Of course, such an attempt is not just a purely academic exercise to satisfy my curiosity or that of my contemporaries. As I have stated, I believe the gospel took shape as an internal document of a community that was experiencing severe tests. That fact does not preclude its becoming a prized document of Christians through the centuries. Some readers may point out that I have overlooked important themes in this gospel. I make no claim to have exhausted its amazing treasury. I have only attempted to take a look at the riches in its vaults. I hope my efforts are not just explications but paths to understanding, avenues that lead to further explorations. If the reading of my meditations sparks reflection and insight into the symbolic universe of some early Christians and helps envision ways to live in the world, my efforts will have been amply rewarded.

1

IN THE BEGINNING WAS THE LOGOS

The claim that the *Logos* incarnate is God comes as a stunning revelation to us at the very beginning of the gospel *According to John*. We have not been prepared for this amazing claim. The gospel does not build up a case for it. Yet we are intrigued by it, wanting to find evidence for it. This quest will demand from us an understanding of the symbolic universe within which the gospel was conceived – a universe with apparently inexhaustible deposits of meaning, undoubtedly worthy of being extracted. All the biblical books, surely, have rich reservoirs of meaning, but this gospel, with its unique claim that the incarnate *Logos* is God, surpasses them all.

The two early Christian hymns included in the New Testament also proclaim that Jesus is the human manifestation of a pre-existent divine being, but they do not assert that he is God. Philippians 2:6 – 11 says that this divine being was "in the form" of God, not God, and that he had no desire for "equality with God." Colossians 1:15 – 20, for its part, describes this being as "the first-born of all creatures," rather than as God.

From beginning to end this book presupposes knowledge of how its language works. On the surface its language appears quite rudimentary, pedestrian, with a rather limited vocabulary. Students of Greek are given their first exercises from the text of *According to John* because of its simplicity. Those who do not become aware soon that this beginner's Greek carries within it many profound levels of meaning, however, are not paying attention to what they are reading.

For Greek Orthodox Christianity and its many daughters, the gospel *According to John* is the canon within the canon. Jesus' bringing eternal life (something human beings have never had but dearly desire) makes possible the "divinization" of Christians. The Son who was glorified on the cross made possible the restoration of the divine image God had originally implanted on Adam, which he lost by sinning. Divinization is the process by which step by step through spiritual retreats and contemplation Christians have the image of God re-implanted on them. For this Christianity the image of God as a baby on his mother's bosom is the central icon. Communion with the icon of the Mother of God and the incarnate God child is paramount. The crucifix, while present in Orthodox churches, is not the center of devotional life. It is in the incarnation, in the *becoming flesh*, that redemption was actualized for those who believe. This is the theme of the whole gospel *According to John*, and I am identifying it at the beginning of my meditations because if one does not know what the gospel is about it is impossible to understand it.

According to John teaches only one doctrine. When it was first proclaimed this doctrine was revolutionary, radical to the extreme, and for proclaiming it the Johannine Christians were misunderstood by other Christians and persecuted by Jews. The one doctrine of this gospel is that Jesus is God, a doctrine that has never lacked those who flatly reject it.

A western Christian who also made this doctrine central, and was also misunderstood by his fellow Christians while alive, was the extraordinary Dane of the nineteenth century, Soren Kierkegaard. He understood well the theme of *According to John,* insisting that what is required is not to accept as God the Risen Christ who has triumphed over death, or the Christ who twenty centuries of Christian theological elaborations proclaims as God, or the one who twenty centuries of western culture presents as the hero of its success. We are not required to recognize as God the Jesus of the miracles, feeding the thousands with a few pieces of bread and fish, walking on water, resurrecting the dead. We are required to recognize as God the Jesus who was the son of Mary and Joseph, a poor carpenter's apprentice who did not look different from any other poor journeyman in Nazareth. Nothing signaled him as distinct, special, worthy of admiration. The Jesus who looks just like the milkman and the baker of the corner — this Jesus is God. Christians must become contemporaries of Jesus and, paradoxically, recognize as God this undistinguished man who looks just like every one else.

Kierkegaard's depiction of Jesus captures what is at the core of *According to John:* Jesus has to be believed as God among us. He is not a man with a privileged divine connection, a blessed man with a double portion of the Spirit. Whether Jesus during his life made open claims to divinity, as this gospel reports, or whether he imposed silence on any one who would make divine claims for him, as the synoptic gospels report, is a matter to be debated. It seems that many people in the first century believed in the existence of gods passing themselves for human beings among them, as Petronius in the *Satyricon* reports. However, it seems to me that most people in that time would have been just as skeptical about the presence of an incarnated god among them as most people are in the twenty-first century. Thus, Kierkegaard's argument is valid: faith is not built on evidence. Of course, if it negates the evidence it may cause psychological damage. To believe is difficult. It requires the intellect to go beyond the evidence.

The gospel *According to Mark* focuses on the passion that culminates in a crucifixion. The journey from Galilee to Jerusalem is staged with three Passion Predictions (Mk. 8:31; 9:31; 10:33 – 34). He is going to Jerusalem to give his life "as a ransom for many" (Mk. 10:45). This declaration is the theological message of *According to Mark. According to John*, on the other hand, idealizes the crucifixion. Its narrative climax is not Jesus' prediction of the crucifixion after the confession of Peter. In fact there are no Passion Predictions, and the confession of Peter is given a totally different content (6:68). Its climax confronts the reader in its first verse,

"In the beginning was the *Logos*, and the *Logos* was with God, and the *Logos* was God" (1:1). A few verses later readers learn that the *Logos* became flesh. They are immediately facing two very technical words: *logos* and *flesh*.

By joining these two words the narrator has superimposed two things which in the rest of the gospel are considered to belong to two quite different worlds. Anticipating the use of Johannine language, the Word, the *Logos* belongs "above," while *flesh* belongs "below." This mismatch creates the tension that informs the rest of the story, and establishes the nature of the problem to be solved by the incarnation.

The theologians of the Hebrew Scriptures had already given a significant role to "the Word of Yahve." The prophets who received "a word of the Lord" understood it as a concrete thing with independent existence. They were mere agents of the transcendent Word of Yahve. In this connection it must be kept in mind that in an oral culture a word has a concrete, if not material, existence. The spoken word is powerful. Once spoken it cannot be retracted. It is like an arrow that has been dispatched from a bow. It cannot be stopped on its tracks by the one speaking. The story of Isaac's blessing of Jacob, much to the dismay of Esau, makes this clear (Gen. 27:33 – 35). The Word of the Lord in the Scriptures, like some other attributes of God, acquired a quasi-independent status. This development was apparently encouraged by the recognition that the ancient anthropomorphic presentations of God were problematic as the Hebraic culture became more reflexive, and heaven and earth were conceived to be further and further apart. As the Wise Man says: "God is in heaven, and you upon earth" (Eccl. 5:2). The distinction of the two realms may not be overlooked. Thus the Wisdom, the Glory, and the Word of Yahve came to be seen as divine agents, or hypostases of God. In the Wisdom Literature, which is quite international in outlook, both the Word and Wisdom are credited with having been the agents of creation (Ps. 33:6; Prov. 8:12, 27 – 30). When the Johannine Christians identified the divine being who became incarnate as *Logos*, they were influenced by the tradition of the Word as the agent of creation, as the linking of *Logos* to "in the beginning" suggests; the following words make this explicit: "all things were made through him, and without him was not anything made that was made" (1:3).

Also, it is quite likely that they understood the philosophical connotations of the word *logos*. In that context, *logos* refers to the capacity to think, to entertain ideas, to express these ideas in words, to construct discourses using words. It is almost indistinguishable from the mind that thinks. The concepts of *reason* and *mind*, it must be noted, are unknown to the authors of the Hebrew Scriptures. Reason and mind are the factors that make human beings, though members of the animal kingdom, different from all other animals. Philosophers of Jesus' time discussed among themselves whether of not there were other animals with *logos*. No doubt some animals distinguish themselves by their intelligence, by their capacity to organize themselves in order to complete a task together. Some animals have their own language and can communicate among themselves. Do they have *logos*? Philo of Alexandria, the most famous Jewish contemporary of Jesus, dedicated a whole treatise, *De animalibus,* to an investigation of this question. As a Jew thoroughly grounded in the Scriptures and a very competent philosopher fully informed in all the currents of thought in which his contemporaries expressed themselves, Philo understood *logos* as that which makes humans capable of participating in the divine.

Logos bridges one of the most formidable philosophical chasms: the line that separates that which is subjective from that which is objective. That is, *logos* makes possible to have an idea in one's mind for which one has not yet found the adequate word. Philosophers distinguished *expressed logos* from *unexpressed logos*. The difference is not that in the second case we have failed to speak a word aloud for others to hear. Rather, the difference is that we have not yet *found* the word which captures the thought we hold in our mind in total subjectivity. We know this experience. More than once we have searched for the right word to express a thought. We considered this one, then that one, and then this other one, and rejected them all because they failed to express the thought we had, but which we did not have the means to express. *Logos* is what holds that thought for which we have not yet found a word in total subjectivity and is the reasoning that conducts the testing that determines the adequacy of different words and eventually matches the subjective thought to its objective expression in the proper word.

As the bridge over the chasm that separates subjectivity from objectivity it is an extremely rich philosophical word. *Logos* is a divine attribute, the ultimate faculty for communication and understanding. God, no doubt, expresses things in the most truthful manner. As *Logos* God is the essence of consciousness and intelligence. With this word, the narrator of *According to John* bridged the gap between the divine and the human. God as God and God as flesh is *Logos*. That is an amazing theological tour de force toward understanding the God who is both hidden in total subjectivity and expressed in humanity.

Besides the astonishing claim that the *Logos* incarnate is God we are given the further claim that Jesus is the *expressed* Logos of the *unexpressed Logos,* but in the rest of the gospel we never again find a personal identification of Jesus as the *Logos*. Thus, after having shocked us with the extraordinary claim that the incarnate *expressed Logos* is God, the gospel does not explicitly connect the One Sent with the *Logos*. Does this indicate that the prologue of the gospel is an addition to an already existing document with an account of Jesus' life? It is a possibility. It is also likely that the members of the Johannine community had no difficulty identifying Jesus, the *Logos,* with the words, the *logos* Jesus spoke to them. As Jews of the first century they were quite aware of the dangers of anthropomorphisms. Thus, the *Logos*, who in the prologue of the gospel is declared to be both God and flesh, is recognized in the words which, as said above, in the Hebraic tradition are taken to be very concrete realities that accomplish the task assigned to them without the possibility of being thwarted. That the Word had been spoken, had been revealed, and had dwelt among humans, creating a way to live in the world, is the message that must be received and believed.

2
Making Himself Equal with God

The temptation with which at the garden of Eden the serpent confronted Eve was to make herself equal to God (Gen 3:5). According to an early Christian hymn, the temptation that the pre-existent Christ confronted and rejected was to make himself equal to God (Phil. 2:6). In the gospel *According to John*, to the contrary, Jesus explicitly accepts as accurate the accusation of making himself equal with God (5:18). This affirmation is at the center of its theology. To begin with, all Christians were Jews who worshipped at the temple of Jerusalem; many of them also belonged to synagogues where they studied the Scriptures and prayed. Because they held this opinion of Jesus, however, they were eventually expelled from the synagogues. Scholars think this happened sometime toward the end of the first century or early in the second.

The story of the man born blind ends with his expulsion from the synagogue (9:34). According to the Pharisees, the one who had been born blind was not only "ex-blind" but also an ex-Jew. The story also tells us that the parents of the ex-blind pleaded ignorance about the details of his life because of their fear of being expelled from the synagogue (9:22). They preferred to ensure their position within the synagogue. Their son preferred to confess what he knew and run the risk of expulsion. In chapter 16 we find another reference to expulsion from the synagogue as the disgrace Christians must be willing to endure for being disciples of Jesus (16:2). We also learn that Joseph of Arimathea was a secret disciple for fear of the Jews (19:38), and that the disciples after the crucifixion were in a room with the door locked "for fear of the Jews" (20:19).

We must note, in this connection, that Paul considered himself a faithful Jew all his life. This shows that the first Christians, who were all Jews, did not think it necessary to cease being Jews in order to be Christians. All Christians were as much Jews as the Pharisees, the Sadducees, the Covenanters of Qumran, the disciples of John (the Baptist), the Nazarites, etc. The temple of Jerusalem was the center that kept all the different Jews, Christians included, living in peace with each other (Acts 2:46; 3:1; 4:1). When it was destroyed by the Romans, Judaism as known until then ceased to be. Only two of its many varieties survived the catastrophe. Pharisaism survived by becoming Rabbinic Judaism, and the Movement of the disciples of Jesus survived by becoming Christianity. Both survivors claimed to be the only legitimate heir to the theological wealth of their religious mother. The struggle for the inheritance caused the two sister religions to engage in an acerbic polemic with disastrous and long-lasting consequences.

The center of the polemic soon came to be occupied by the only doctrine in Judaism. The Judaism of the Jerusalem temple and Rabbinic Judaism distinguish themselves by being religions of observance, not of doctrine. The exception that proves the rule is monotheism. While the temple built by Solomon stood, the people of Jerusalem worshipped many gods. At the altar of the Jerusalem temple sacrifices to Asherah, Moloch and other deities were offered frequently with royal sponsorship. In the neighboring countryside, the people frequented the groves and the high places where sacrifices to Baal (the god of the storm that brings rain) were offered, and they were routinely involved in sacred prostitution to insure the fertility of the flocks and the fields. After the destruction of that temple in 586 BCE, the prophetic traditions of the Word of Yahve, now alive in the voices of Jeremiah, Ezekiel and the disciples of Isaiah of Jerusalem, gained the attention of the people with arguments that denied the existence of any god other than Yahve. Thus Israelite religion re-invented itself as the paragon of monotheism.

This doctrine became central to the religion of the Second Temple, dedicated in 515 BCE and destroyed in 70 CE.

The dispersion of the Jews during and after the Exile in Babylon saw the emergence of a new institution which may have had roots in the Exile: the synagogue. Deuteronomic traditions established that only the altar at the temple in Jerusalem was the legitimate place where sacrifices were to be offered, but access to it was not always available due to its distance from where Jews were now living. At the synagogues, the Torah, the document being compiled at that time by the priests, became the center of attention. The Torah, however, was not studied in order to establish right doctrines, or a creed. It was studied to map a way of life. Obedience to the commandments became the way to live in harmony with God. The scribes, a new class of experts on Torah, adopted as the motto of the synagogue the *Shema*, the text from *Deuteronomy* that became the call to worship: "Hear, O Israel: Yahve is our God, Yahve is One" (Det. 6:4). Its centrality was recognized by Christians who in the gospel *According to Mark* report that Jesus included the *Shema* as part of the great commandment to love God with all your heart, mind and soul (Mk 12:29).

In *According to John* we find a Jesus who is viewed by "the Jews" as one who breaks the law of the Sabbath and, therefore, is a sinner (9:24); he also blasphemes by "making himself equal with God" (5:18). On account of this preposterous claim, "the Jews" thought it impossible for Christians to claim the inheritance of the monotheistic religion of the Second Temple. As far as they could tell, these Christians had a second god.

The prologue concludes stating that the Son is "in the bosom of the Father" (1:18). This metaphor underlines the intimacy of the relationship with a very feminine touch. Jesus himself declares that "the Father is in me and I am in the Father" (10:38). To Philip he explains that whoever has seen him has seen the Father (14:9). In a more direct statement Jesus affirms, "I and the Father are one" (10:30). At the end, Thomas makes the confession that the Johannine Christians thought all Christians should make: "My Lord and my God" (20:28). In Chapter 17 Jesus appeals to the unity enjoyed by the Father and him and insists that there must be unity among the disciples. At the climax of the prayer Jesus pleads: "as thou, Father, art in me, and I in thee, that they also may be one in us: that the world may believe that thou hast sent me" (17:21).

That the unity of the Father and the Son is open to allow the disciples, already united among themselves, to enter it and be united "in us," tells us that the unity of the Father and the Son does not imply homogeneity. There can be differences among those united. The next verse says that the glory of the Son was given to him by the Father (17:22). The relationship of the Father and the Son is that of "The One Who Sends" and "The One Sent." To see the relationship in this way is what not only the disciples but the whole world must come to see. All must recognize in him the One Sent by the Father. In this way the declaration that The Son is God, totally repugnant to Judaism, is already being nuanced in *According to John*.

It took a couple of centuries for Christianity to fully accept the idea that Jesus was not another incarnate divine being, but the incarnation of God. That was done at the Council of Nicea in 325 CE. Not all Christians shared this way of seeing Jesus however, especially those who were primarily influenced by the preaching of Paul as evidenced by the gospel *According to Mark*. Justin Martyr, in his *Dialogue with Trypho the Jew*, is the one who about 150 CE brought to the forefront the Johannine understanding of the *Logos* as the key to Christology. His arguments were then developed by Athanasius, the one who proposed a *Logos*/God Christology at Nicea. The position of Arius, who insisted on seeing the divine being incarnated in Jesus as a "first-born" or one "begotten," however, did not disappear after Nicea. Arian Christianity continued to be prominent in the West for many centuries even after the Council of Chalcedon, in 451 CE, arrived at a compromised explanation of how the *Logos* and God could be one. The long history of the Christological controversies in the first Christian centuries actually begins with the Johannine community's recognition that by claiming that the *Logos* was God they had a problem on their hands if they wished to remain monotheistic. That it saw the problem is evident by its effort to give some nuance to its claim to Jesus' equality with God.

In chapter 5, where "the Jews" explicitly accuse Jesus of making himself equal with God, Jesus defends himself by explaining that while in fact the Son and the Father are one, his claim to divinity does not represent a real challenge to monotheism. In order to understand this defense of monotheism we need to consider some background. Judaism taught that while God did delegate some functions to agents, there were some functions that were exclusively God's. These were primarily the prerogatives to judge and to give life. After having healed the paralytic at the pool of Bethesda, Jesus claims these two divine prerogatives for himself.

In their discussions of the person of God, the Pharisees were also concerned with how to understand God's need to keep God's laws. This was a problem in connection with the Sabbath law. Since the world does not run on its own and there are no other gods in charge of running different natural phenomena, if God rests on Sabbaths, creation should disintegrate on these days. Since creation continues to function properly on Sabbaths, God must be working on every Sabbath to keep it going. This means that God also has the prerogative to work on Sabbath.

Jesus shocked "the Jews" by claiming to have this prerogative also. To defend himself for having cured the paralytic and having told him to carry his mat home on a Sabbath, Jesus says: "My Father works until now, and I work" (5:17). "The Jews," correctly, understood that with these words Jesus was claiming for himself God's exclusive prerogative to work on Sabbath. This declaration explicitly divides God in two and claims that both can work on Sabbath.

The conflict over monotheism is elaborated in *According to John* in two directions. On the one hand, Jesus elevates his claims even higher. Besides the prerogative to work on the Sabbath, the Son can also judge (5:22, 27), and he can give life "to whomever he wishes" (5:21, 26). Both activities, as already said, are God's exclusive prerogatives. On the other hand, the Son cannot exercise these prerogatives independently. Everything he does, he does together with, and according to the will of the Father (5:19, 30). His activity is totally subordinated to the Father. He does not have an independent will. In this way the Son as God is being carefully defined as subject to the Father's will. *According to John*, the gospel that squarely challenges the monotheistic religion of Yahve, begins the process that Christianity has been carrying on for centuries: trying to explain the relationships of the persons within the Godhead in a way that does not negate its claim to have only one God.

The claim that the incarnate *Logos* is God is so audacious that *According to John* recognizes that this claim needs to be backed by evidence. At once, Jesus admits that his claim cannot be sustained by the fact that he says so. "If I bear witness to myself, my testimony is not true" (5:31). To sustain his claim to God's exclusive prerogatives and to work as one with the Father, Jesus presents supporting witnesses.

The first is John the Baptist. His ministry had been "a burning and shining lamp" which for some time the Jews had considered valid (5:35). In the first chapter we read that "John bore witness to him .... he confessed, he did not deny .... 'I have seen and have borne witness that this is the Son of God'" (1:15, 20, 34). Given his influence in Judaism, the testimony of John is effective. But his repeated negations ("I am not the Christ," "I am not Elijah," "I am not the prophet," etc., 1:21 – 22) and the rivalry between the disciples of John and those of Jesus (given that Jesus was baptizing more people than John, 3:26; 4:2) gave rise to doubts about John's testimony among some. Jesus, therefore, presents more witnesses.

In the second place, Jesus appeals to "the works which the Father has granted me to accomplish." They testify that he is the One Sent by the Father (5:36). In this gospel his works are designated "signs." At the end of the gospel the narrator tells us that Jesus performed "many signs in the presence of the disciples, which are not written in this book; but these are written that you may believe that Jesus is the Christ, the Son of God, and that believing you may have life in his name" (20:30 – 31). The testimony of the signs, it is argued, should be sufficient to produce faith and life. Throughout the gospel there are reports of people who believed on account of the signs, but also of those who failed to see the sign value of the works of Jesus. This, it would seem, makes the testimony of his works ambiguous.

Appeal is then made to the most important One who also bears witness: "the One who sent me, the Father." God's testimony should prove irrefutable. The problem is that those who demand proofs of authenticity for Jesus' claims "have never heard God's voice or seen God's appearance" (5:37). This is the tragic condition of those who do not see the Father in the person of the One Sent by the Father (5:38). Thus, the testimony that should be incontrovertible is beyond the reach of those who ask for it.

The situation becomes even worst when those seeking eternal life look for it in the wrong place. Instead of coming to Jesus to obtain it, they misguidedly search the Scriptures hoping to find it there. The function of Scripture is not to give life. It is to bear witness to Jesus (5:38). Once again a testimony that should be effective is wasted by those who misunderstand the purpose of the Scriptures. Their real problem, actually, is that due to their pride in the Scriptures they lack the love of God (5:42-44).

Chapter 5 ends in a way similar to that of chapter 9. The irony of the situation is, again, on the surface. Those seeking eternal life in the Scriptures are not condemned by the One Sent by the Father, who was sent with the specific purpose of giving life, and also has the authority to judge. They consider Moses to be the great mediator between God and the people. On the basis of Deut. 18:15 – 18, they are waiting for the appearance of the prophet "like Moses." "The Jews" will suffer a great disappointment, however. Having "placed their hope" in Moses, they are actually being condemned by Moses, not realizing that the Scriptures, instead of being the source of life, are witness to the validity of his claim to be one with the Father. As is said laconically in the prologue, the law was given through Moses, grace and truth are alive in Jesus Christ (1:17). It is indeed a great tragedy when people reject the One Who is God's Grace and Truth incarnate because they have placed their hopes on the one who met God at the top of Mt. Sinai. By judging Jesus' claim to be blasphemy on the basis of the Scriptures, "the Jews" are under the power of the Scriptures to condemn.

No doubt the Johannine Christians who made the absolute claim that the *Logos* is God, but who also saw the need to establish some parameters to that claim, had a great sense of irony. Their ironic frame of mind and the subtlety with which they nuance the relationship of the Father and the Son as one tell us that the Johannine community had a sophisticated literary sense. It is quite amazing to see how the world of village life exhibited in the oral traditions of Jesus' sayings, where shepherds chase after sheep, women bake bread and plowmen work their fields, in just a few years became a highly literary language where arguments are built according to philosophical models and ironic double meanings take the stage. Early Christians soon learned how to express their faith in language that was understandable and appealing to different publics, and felt quite free to do so. It was only because of these skills that they could make and sustain their claim that the incarnate Son was equal with God.

3

HE WHO FOLLOWS ME ... WILL HAVE THE LIGHT OF LIFE

The prologue of *According to John* concludes by presenting a rationale for the gospel: "No one has ever seen God" (1:18). The Old Testament tells us that Adam and Eve saw and conversed with God in Eden, and Ex. 24:9 – 11 says that Moses, Nadab, Abihu and seventy Israelites saw and ate with God on the top of Mount Sinai. But here these reports are set aside, and a new solution to this problem is advanced. The situation now is different because the means for seeing and knowing God are now available: "the only Son, who is in the bosom of the Father, he has made Him known." The mission of the *Logos* on earth is not necessarily to die in order to redeem humanity. His purpose is to reveal the God no one has ever seen.

The prologue has already told us that "in him was life, and the life was the light of men. The light shines in the darkness, and the darkness has not apprehended it" (1:4 – 5). Here we have the plot of this gospel in a nutshell, and the first of its many double entendres. In Greek just one verb says both to comprehend and to apprehend. Whether the thing is grabbed by the mind or by the hand is to be determined by the context.

It is a physical reality that the light of the weakest of matches triumphs over the darkness surrounding it. It is impossible for darkness to eradicate the light of a single match. Light always triumphs over darkness. What is true in the physical world is also true in the spiritual world. Those who are of the darkness neither comprehend nor apprehend the *Logos*. This is the drama of the Fourth Gospel. Several times we read that his listeners do not comprehend what Jesus says to them (10:6, 39; 16:18), and when the authorities send their agents to apprehend him, they return empty handed (7:44; 8:20; 10:31; 11:57). At the garden on the other side of the Kidron brook the soldiers who come to take him prisoner fall back to their backs to the ground when Jesus takes the initiative and identifies himself saying, "I am he." Judas has no chance to give him a treasonous kiss (18:1 – 8). On one occasion, when all those around him wish to kill him and pick up stones to do so, Jesus simply walks through them and leaves the city, and no one throws a single stone (8:59). As the light, he cannot be snatched by the forces of darkness.

Finding a man who was born blind, Jesus declares: "While I am in the world, I am the light of the world." Nothing can prevent the effectiveness of the presence of the Light. The Light reveals the God no one has ever seen, but to see Him it is necessary to believe. To see and to believe in the Johannine language are synonyms. Thus, as the prologue has already announced, the benefit of the Light to those who believe is to receive the life in it. In other words, the revelation of God made possible by the incarnation does not bring to the world information about God or the future of the world. It brings something incommensurably more valuable: eternal life. The light of the Son does not make possible knowledge; it transmits life.

The Jesus of *According to John* at times appears obtuse demanding faith without providing the information that would support faith. His proclamation consists of "I am … " Among these sayings we find: "I am the light of the world" (8:12). The Light enlightens those who believe God is in Jesus and imparts life to them. To believe the Light, to be children of Light (12:36), is to recognize the

One Sent by the Father. Said in a different way, to believe in him is to believe in "The One Who Sent Me."

Those confronted by the Light find themselves in an inevitable crisis. They must make a judgment about the Light. Those who see and believe that the Light is the One Sent by the Father receive eternal life. Those who do not see the connection between the One Sent and the One Sending are immediately condemned. The coming of the Light to the world divides those confronted by the Light into believers and unbelievers (9:16).

In Greek, nouns are characterized by their endings. Changing the ending of a verbal root changes its meaning. In this case, the root *kri* may take the ending *sis* and mean "the act of judging, the carrying out of a judgment." If it is given the ending *ma* it means "the result of a judgment, a sentence," implying that the sentence is negative, a condemnation. Having to judge, having to make a decision creates an internal crisis.

Those who come face to face with the Light find themselves in a crisis. They have to decide whether Jesus is God or a blasphemer. On more than one occasion Jesus explains that he did not come to condemn, but to save the world. No doubt, that was his purpose. But the reality is that his very presence in the world results in the judgment of the world. While some are benefiting from the Light, seeing, believing and receiving eternal life, others do not see, do not believe and are condemned.

More tragic than the condition of those who do not see is that of those who, on the basis of confidence in their ability to see, judge Jesus a blasphemer. This is the condition of "the Jews" who use the Scriptures as the source of light and who on this basis judge Jesus and condemn him as a sinner who is anything but one sent by the Father. This is the theme of the healing of the man born blind. The story says that Jesus made mud and anointed the eyes of the blind with it. Then he sent him to the pool of Siloam. The name of the pool comes from the Hebrew word *Shalom*, peace. The narrator twists the etymology of the word and explains to the reader that the name comes from the Hebrew *Shalach*, meaning "Sent." After washing his eyes with the water of The One Sent, the man born blind now sees. This is a never-heard-of miracle, as the blind man informs the Pharisees. It has never been done before (9:32).

As an afterthought, after we have read the story, the narrator informs us that the miracle took place on a Sabbath. Basing themselves on Torah, the Pharisees condemn Jesus *in absentia* as a sinner. Since it was not an emergency case, he could well have waited until the following day to make the mud and anoint the eyes of the blind.

The readers are emphatically informed that the Pharisees judge Jesus a sinner on the basis of their knowledge. "We know that this man is a sinner" (9:24). "We know that God has spoken to Moses" (9:29). On the contrary, both the parents and the man born blind confess that they do not know (9:12, 21, 25).

Actually, the man born blind confesses that he knows one thing: he was blind and now he sees (9:25). What he knows he knows from experience. What the Pharisees know they know from authority. They are proud disciples of Moses, and according to the Pharisaic interpretation of the law of Moses anyone who makes mud and anoints another with it on a Sabbath has broken the law and is a sinner. By experience the ex- blind testifies that the Light of the Sent One facilitates seeing and gives life. Those who think they have found life in the Scriptures, on the other hand, are blinded by their own self sufficiency. In this context Jesus says: "For judgment (*krima*= condemnation) I came into this world, that those who do not see may see, and that those who see may become blind" (9:39).

This story was put together by those who knew what they were doing. They built its plot to highlight the irony of the situation – irony being a characteristic of most Johannine stories. Those who think themselves to be well informed and able judges end up judged and condemned. Those who know and feel secure in their beliefs are declared to be blind sinners. In the meantime, the one who was born blind has his eyes open to see, and without becoming an idolater adores the Sent One who gave him Light (9:38).

The spark in the half closed eyes and the intelligent smile of the narrator is visible to readers through the ages. The blinding certainty of those who pretend to see is exposed for what it is when confronted by the Light of the world. Seeing God in the Son who came to reveal God cannot depend on other sources of light. Those who rely on them end up revealing that they are in the dark.

The presence of Jesus gives light to the one born blind and blinds those who think they see. As the headlights of a car allow the driver to see the road ahead but blind those who travel in the opposite direction, so the Light of the world illumines those who see by his Light and blinds those who insist on seeing by their own lights.

In this gospel the message of Jesus is not centered on the establishment of the Kingdom of God. What Jesus reveals is the source of life. The one born blind, as the Pharisees say, is a disciple of the One who gave him sight. Actually, for the Johannine community he is the prototype of the true disciple. Once able to see he worships the unique God who gave him light and life. His eyes were washed in the fountain of The One Sent by God. This is how the *Logos* makes visible the God no one has ever seen. As the Sent One insists, he did not come to condemn the world but to save it, but at the same time, unavoidably, he blinds and condemns those who pretend to see, especially the disciples of Moses.

The coming of the Light divides the world between those who abide in darkness and those who walk in the Light (3:19; 11:9 – 10; 12:35, 46). *According to John* distinguishes itself by giving the world a radically dualistic structure, but its dualism has lost the temporal tension that informs the expectations of a coming kingdom which are characteristic of apocalypticism. In *According to John* we have the repetition of the first day of creation — *in the beginning*. Once again the light that brings about life displaces the darkness that lurks in the waters of the deep (Gen. 1:1 – 2). The tensions created by the Johannine dualisms provide the context for its understanding of salvation. That the light enlightens and blinds, gives life and condemns to death causes one to wonder how this can be. Did Jesus come to bring life or to bring judgment? To collapse the apocalyptic final judgment into the appearance of the Son as the revealer of the Father only increases the tension that has always existed within the view that God is both a loving Creator and a Judge. This is the tension that sustains faith. To believe on the basis of the Light that emanates from Jesus is the opposite of unbelief, but this is not in tension with the unbelief that characterizes the darkness. While the darkness may seem threatening it is unable to comprehend or apprehend the light. The Light of the world that brings life eternal illumines the lives of those who believe and takes away from them all fear of the darkness. The children of light don't live for the future and have nothing to fear from the future. The Light has given them eternal life.

4

No One Has Ascended into Heaven

The prophets of Israel gave to Western Civilization its orientation toward the future. They were the ones who diagnosed the need for a radical change from the *status quo* and predicted that this change would come in the future. Traditional societies were anchored in the annual natural cycle. Life was to be lived in conformity with the constant repetition of the vital cycle in nature. The prophets freed time from the notion that it is bound to the cycles of nature with their constant returns to the beginning. They conceived time as a horizontal line into the future that would bring The Day of the Lord and The Kingdom of God. To live is to hope for That Great Day, not to reenact the past *ad infinitum* in yearly festivals.

Rather than to think of life as grounded in time and history, Plato taught that to live in the accidents of time and its changes is to live anxiously, lacking a footing in reality. To live authentically is not to become but to be. To live wisely is to anchor one's life on that which *is,* not on the things that are constantly *becoming* something else. To live is to escape the world of becoming in time and take hold of the things that are eternal. It is, therefore, absolutely necessary to gain knowledge of the things that are in the higher spheres of the chain of being. The scaffolding of life is not in time but in space. About the things that exist in time and are constantly becoming something else one may have an *opinion*. To *know* is to have grasped intellectually the things that are, that are not changed by time. Truth should not be confused with opinions about material things. The truth only exists in that which is eternal, that is, in ideas.

As a Mediterranean nation, the Jews of Jesus' time were thoroughly Hellenized. Even if the common people may not have known Plato's philosophical work, and may not even have known his name, the Hellenistic world was permeated with a popular version of Plato's thought. This meant that the prophetic vision, which instilled hope in a future when communion with God would be possible as God's kingdom became a reality and God's throne was located on Mount Zion, was not predominant. Within a Hellenistic culture Jews explored the mystical avenues used by Hellenistic mystery cults, and Merkabah Judaism developed its own version of how to ascend to the heavenly spheres in order to get in touch with the divine realities that are eternal.

Jewish Merkabah mysticism established ways of ascending to the heavenly spheres and anchoring one's life on the things that really are. Not surprisingly, Elijah's chariot (2 Kings 2:11) became the vehicle of choice for those who wished to ascend to the heavenly regions and thus escape from the anxieties of life in the changes brought by time to those living in matter. Even the human body was an impediment to the ascent to spiritual realities. That trips to heaven provided knowledge of heavenly realities is also in evidence in the *Revelation of John the Theologian*. He reports to have ascended and been admitted to the very room where God's throne and God's entourage are to be found. There he learned things that were sealed, were to remain secret, until the proper time (Rev 4:1 – 6:1). The apostle Paul confesses to having ascended to the third heaven and to Paradise. There he was told things "that cannot be told, which man may not utter" (2 Cor. 12:1 – 4).

In Platonic terms reaching the higher spheres and seeing and hearing things that are secret can only be realized by the soul, or the intellect, the mind. In the Hebraic traditional culture the body is essential to any form of life. Matter is not ballast that must be discharged by those who wish to reach higher forms of reality. It is essential to any living thing. Thus Paul, a Jew to the core, as an intelligent citizen of the Hellenized world, having achieved an ascent to Paradise, wonders whether he was in the body or out of the body during this journey to the world above. To a Platonist the body would constitute a disqualifying impediment. An apocalyptic Jew like Paul had difficulty conceiving how he could make a trip to heaven without his body. Admirably, Paul admits his ignorance as whether he made the trip in the body or without it (2 Cor. 12:3).

The gospel *According to John* has some passing references to the need to wait for the future and its drastic changes. This gospel makes five references to "the resurrection in the last day" (6:39, 40, 44, 54; 11:24). The predominant perspective in this gospel, however, is not temporal; it is spatial, vertical and challenging. "No one has ascended into heaven, but he who descended from heaven" (3:13). The admonition is not "to watch and wait," as in the synoptic gospels, or the letters of Paul. *According to John* does not advise having patience, or resignation until the Day of the Lord. It also contradicts all those who claim to have ascended to the heavenly spheres. The flat declaration that "no one has ascended to heaven" must have been quite shocking, both for the mystery religions whose devotees were initiated for these journeys and for a Judaism, whether apocalyptic or mystical, that also prepared people for journeys to the realms above.

While affirming that no one has ever ascended to heaven, *According to John* cites one exception to the rule. The One Sent by the Father, who descended from heaven, has also ascended into heaven. In other words, the one who descended to the world "below" has ascended to the world "above" from which he came. For those who are from below it is impossible to ascend. Only he who descended from "above" has ascended.

The world above and the world below are also designated "the spirit" and "the flesh." These two realities are, apparently, mutually exclusive. "That which is born of the flesh is flesh, and that which is born of the spirit is spirit" (3:6). Since human beings are born of the flesh, they belong to the world below; therefore, it is impossible for them to ascend. The Father's purpose in sending his Son to this world was to open up the world above, where eternal life is the norm, to those born below. In other words, the Son of Man descended only to ascend. His authorization to ascend resides in his origin in the world above. Those from below are, on this account, destined to die and remain below.

In a confrontation with "the Jews" during the Feast of Tabernacles, Jesus says to them: "I go away, and you will seek me but die in your sin; where I am going you cannot come .… You are from below, I am from above; you are of this world, I am not of this world. Therefore, I told you that you would die in your sins" (8:21 – 24). To have been born below, to have been born of the flesh, is to have to die in one's sins. The mission of the Son is to "become flesh" (not to "be born in the flesh") (1:14) to release the constraints that separate the world below from the world above. The basic fact of life below has been altered. Eternal life, the norm of the world above, is now available in the world below since the one who ascended into heaven has opened the world above to those living in the world below.

Of course, in the opinion of "the Jews" Jesus' origin is from below. They know perfectly well who his parents are. They ask themselves, "Is not this Jesus, the son of Joseph, whose father and mother we know? How does he now say, 'I have come down from heaven?'" (6:42). Knowing that even his disciples are perturbed by his claim to have descended from heaven, Jesus asks them: "Then what if you were to see the Son of Man ascending where he was before?" (6:62). Apparently his ascent will be more extraordinary, more spectacular, more revealing than his descent. His ascent is the exception.

Every reader of this gospel must answer the question "the Jews," almost pleading, ask him: "Who are you?" (8:25). Pilate asks the more specific question: "Where are you from?" (19:9). Frustrated by Jesus' silence, Pilate threatens him: "You will not speak to me? Do you not know that I have authority to release you, and authority to crucify you?" With this claim to authority the evangelist highlights the irony of the situation. Jesus now informs Pilate: "You would have no authority over me unless it had been given you from above" (19:10 – 11). As a person in the world below Jesus may be subject to the power of Rome. His precarious standing before Pilate, however, is in reality authorized by the Power that comes from above. His death below is not the triumph of the power that has its sources below. He belongs to the world above, as he said, "I am from above" (8:23).

In spite of the persistent efforts of "the Jews" to kill him, they cannot achieve their purpose because Jesus cannot die stoned by "the Jews." He must die the Roman way, by crucifixion. His exit from the world below must be an ascent, an elevation. The Son of man must be lifted up. "When you have lifted up the Son of man, then you will know that I am" (8:28). The question of "the Jews," "Who are you?" here receives its answer, "I am." If his incarnation was his descent, his death is to be his ascension. The post on which he will be "lifted up" is the road on which he will journey to heaven.

The turning point in Jesus' ministry is precipitated by some Greeks who provide a contrast to the attitude of "the Jews" who neither see nor believe. When Jesus finds out that some Greeks have said: "We wish to see Jesus" (12:21), he reacts by announcing: "The hour has come for the Son of man to be glorified" (12:23). Then he explains: "And I, when I am lifted up from the earth, will draw all men to myself" (12:32). The narrator then explains: "He said this to show by what death he was to die." As could be expected, those who heard Jesus' explanation did not understand it. They asked: "How can you say that the Son of man must be lifted up?" (12:34). The lifting up of the Son of man is not an option; it is a necessity. He "must be lifted up," or, as said by Pilate, "crucified" or, as Jesus said it, "glorified." He is the exception who is glorified by his ascent to heaven.

In this gospel these words describe the completion of Jesus' mission. He accomplishes it by returning to the Father "crucified," "lifted up," "glorified." This is the way by which he returns to the world above from which he came. As Jesus says, "I came from the Father …. and [I am] going to the Father" (16:28). Those who know this know who he is and where he is from.

This is known by faith. Only faith makes it possible to recognize the Father as the origin and the destiny of the One who dies "lifted up" and in this way ascends to where he came from. Faith, however, must always rest on an object. Faith must be on something specific. Faith cannot be based on a mist without contours and attributes. It is not a feeling, or an intuition without specificity. The Son of Man must be crucified to provide the object faith requires. Therefore, when the Greeks express the wish to *see* Jesus, he knows that the hour for him to become the object on which faith is to be tested has arrived. Only when he is "lifted up" can he "draw all men" to himself. He is to be lifted up "so that whosoever believes in him may have eternal life."

The central metaphor of *According to John* is offered by Jesus to Nicodemus: "As Moses lifted up the serpent in the wilderness, so must the Son of Man be lifted up" (3:14). The image of Moses lifting up a post with a bronze serpent on it as a way of giving life to the Israelites who were dying in the desert bitten by serpents (Num. 21:9) is given as the best way to understand the crucifixion of Jesus. The bronze serpent in the wilderness was not itself the effective antidote against the venom of the desert reptiles, it was, rather, the vision of the lifted shining object that counteracted the poison.

The central theological text of this gospel is not 3:16. It is 3:14 – 15: "As Moses lifted up the serpent in the wilderness, so must the Son of Man be lifted up that whosoever believes in him may have eternal life." Human beings don't need to ascend to heaven. They received life by seeing the one who ascended, who was lifted up. Thereby they receive eternal life. Those who according to Merkabah Judaism ascended to the realms above expected to see there things about which they could not speak after their return to earth. By their ascent they had gained esoteric information which they could not share. *According to John* makes the point that those who see the Son of man lifted up receive eternal life, rather than new knowledge. As a result they are to become witnesses of life. They must share their life with others and thus promote life. This gospel offers in this way an argument against those who claim to be in possession of visions or revelations that give them esoteric, secret knowledge.

This is the Gospel of the gospel *According to John*: to believe in the One who was lifted up to show the love of the Father, from whom he came and to whom he is going, is to be drawn to the one who ascended. To believe in the one who was "lifted up," the only one who "ascended into heaven" is to "be born from above." What Jesus provides believers is not knowledge, but life, even while living in the world below.

In the dialogue with Nicodemus, Jesus informs him that it is necessary for him to "be born *anothen*." Once again we encounter here the irony of this evangelist. *Anothen* is a Greek word with double meanings. The context alone can tell us how to understand it.

As is to be expected in a dialogue in this gospel, what Jesus says is misunderstood by his interlocutor – it does not matter with whom he is speaking. Nicodemus imagines that he must be born again "from his mother's womb," what nonsense! Jesus is telling him that he must be born from above of "the Spirit" (3:5). This is necessary because those who are from below, those who are of the flesh, live in a world where death is the ultimate certainty. Birth from above is the birth of faith, and the Son of Man came to provide the definitive object on which faith must rest. What women and men must see is not what they are anxious to see in journeys to the higher spheres. Seeing the Son lifted up brings about a birth "from above." The higher spheres are not opened to those who climb on Elijah's chariot, as Merkabah mysticism promised. Eternal life, the life of the higher spheres is accessible now only because the ascent of the Son on the cross.

The Prologue has already said it in a nutshell: "To all who received him, who believed in his name, he gave power to become children of God; who were born, not of blood nor of the will of the flesh nor of the will of man, but of God" (1:12–13). Here we are told different ways to be born below and one way to be born "from above" (*anothen*). Since we live twenty centuries later it is difficult to distinguish with any certainty the three ways one can be born from below. I can offer only tentative suggestions.

To be born of blood may refer to birth from a tribal marriage. To be born of the will of the flesh may refer to birth from a passionate sexual encounter. To be born of the will of a husband (*andros*) may refer to birth from the need of the husband to have descendants, particularly among those with a tribal mentality. These are the ways in which people are born in the world below. Those who believe in his name, those who see the Son lifted up, are empowered, authorized children of God, because, as a matter of fact, they are "born of God." Such are no longer from below. They are born of the Spirit, born from above. In the same way in which a flag lifted up on its pole draws together a people and constitutes it a nation, the Son of Man lifted up on a cross draws toward himself all who believe and constitutes them "born of God."

Those who are born from above, even while in the realm below, are not confined to the realm below. Their faith makes them live in eternal life. Only those whose origin is from above can participate in the glory of the one who was lifted up and glorified. The cross that lifts up the Son offers the object on which faith must rest. The object of faith is not doctrinal knowledge. It is seeing the Son on the cross ascending to the Father who sent him. The Son who is lifted up is the way, the only means of access to the heavenly regions. As a means of transportation that makes possible the ascent to the Father who causes us to be born from above and gives us eternal life, Elijah's chariot is no competition to the Son of Man who was glorified on a cross.

5
OF HIS FULLNESS WE HAVE ALL RECEIVED

Of all the books of the New Testament the one that is closest to *According to John* is the letter *To the Colossians*. More specifically, the prologue of the gospel and the hymn that serves as the text on which the author of the letter builds his argument have similar views and concerns. In both documents there is an argument against those who wish to escape the earthly realm by means of ascensions on the chain of being.

By stating that "no one has ascended into heaven," *According to John* is attacking Merkabah Judaism and its mystic journeys to higher spheres of the cosmos, as pointed out in the previous meditation. Such journeys were also promoted by the popular mystery cults at the time. In the gospel there is only one exception to the rule. It is the ascent of the Son who descended in the first place. His crucifixion, his being lifted up or glorified, means not only that he has ascended into heaven; it also means that the body of the Risen Christ is the temple (2:21) of a new cosmos of the Spirit. As does *According to John*, *To the Colossians* also builds an argument against a Christianity that preaches a mystical path to a perfection that is achieved through trips through the spheres. In preparation for such trips prospective travelers must do ascetic exercises and initiation rites into esoteric knowledge of the "principalities and powers" of the air (Col. 2:10, 14). The desire for these journeys was caused by the sense that the earth is not the natural human home. On it humans are foreigners. Here they are sojourners from their true home. Thus, the soul's desire is to return to its real home in the higher spheres.

According to John and *To the Colossians* not only share a concern to disconnect Christianity from the wide-spread belief that the divine was to be reached through mystical ascents; they also tie salvation to creation in a strikingly creative way. The cross is not presented as the culmination of Jesus' life in terms of cultic sacrifices. It is understood, rather, using metaphors about creation. Let's consider first the hymn quoted by the author of *To the Colossians*:

> He is the image of the invisible God,
> The first born of every creature.
> By him were all things created.
> He is the Head of the Body.
> He is the beginning,
> The first born of the dead.
> By him were all things reconciled.
> In him the *Pleroma* is pleased to dwell.
> (reconstructed from Col. 1:15 – 20)

This early Christian hymn has much in common with the prologue of the gospel, which some scholars think is also built on an early Christian hymn. Both documents share a vision of creation that is uniquely Christian. Both see the divine being who achieved salvation as the divine agent who brought about creation. They identify this divine agent differently, but the language has a common background. Both the "image" (*eikon*) and the *Logos* were conceived to be hypostases of God with specific capabilities and functions, as noticed in our first meditation. *To the Colossians* considers this divine agent a divine being. *According to John* greatly raises the stakes and claims he is God.

It may also be noted that while in the gospel "in the beginning" is a clear echo to that never-never time when creation took place, in the Colossian hymn the Risen Christ is designated "the Beginning." This represents a peculiar Christological move. That the hymn identified the agent of creation as the Image is understandable because the report that the first pair of human beings was created in the image of God had already given rise to speculations as to what this meant, and has continued to do so till this day. An image is, no doubt, something visible. Both the hymn and the prologue say that God is invisible, or that no one has ever seen God, and both also say that the Image, or the Son, has made God known (1:18).

The *Genesis* account of creation says that "God created man in his own image, in the image of God he created him: male and female he created them" (Gn. 1:27). As the image of God within creation, the male and female "man" were the "stand-ins" for a God who had created the world from outside and remained outside the created world. By identifying Jesus Christ as the Image he is seen as the representative of God within creation. By choosing to speak of the *Logos* rather than the *eikon* as the basic metaphor, *According to John* takes advantage of the richer connotations of *Logos* in the Hellenistic philosophical tradition, as already noticed in our first meditation. Both the Image and the *Logos* are used to concretize God within the world.

Another feature shared by the gospel and the letter is that both distance themselves from the Torah, while being in close dependence upon its stories and basic theological vision. The letter is concerned with the desire for perfection. This is also a concern of the gospel *According to Matthew* (Mt. 5:48; 19:21), but while in this gospel perfection is related to Torah, the letter makes no reference to the law at all. The gospel *According to John*, on the other hand, is concerned with eternal life and relegates the law to "the Jews." In these two documents Moses and the law are either ignored or considered irrelevant to the attainment of perfection or of eternal life.

Most significantly and especially to be noticed is that both of these more or less contemporary documents refer to the Risen Christ as the *Pleroma,* the Fullness, the Plenitude. The hymn affirms that after "all things" (*ta panta*) were reconciled in him, the *Pleroma* is pleased to dwell in him. Two things must be emphasized about this. One is that the verb used here is not the one used by the gospel to describe the dwelling of the *Logos* in the flesh. The dwelling of the *Pleroma* in "him" is a settling down, the taking up of residence: *katoikein*. This declaration of the hymn is then expanded by the author of the letter saying that "in him the whole *Pleroma* of deity dwells bodily" (2:9). Here the *Pleroma* is defined as "the fullness of deity," and the dwelling is characterized as "bodily." This is a most striking image of the cosmic Christ. The body of the divine Risen Christ is the *Pleroma,* that is, the totality of the universe.

The *Pleroma* is the fullness of "all things," which the hymn tells us were created and reconciled by Christ. According to the explanatory expansion of the text of the hymn provided by the author of the letter, these include all things "visible and invisible, whether thrones or dominions or principalities or authorities, all things were created through him and for him. He is before all things and in him all things hold together" (Col. 1:16 – 17). In similar fashion the prologue of the gospel tells us that "all things were made through him, and without him was not anything made that was made" (1:3). The creation, the conglomerate of all things made, together with the creator God, is called the *Pleroma*, the Fullness. This term encompasses all that is, including, of course, the being of God.

The word *Pleroma* named what the philosophers conceived as the totality of all that exists, and both the letter and the gospel either refer to the Risen Christ as the *Pleroma,* or that the *Pleroma* is pleased to dwell in the Risen Christ. There is no better way to identify the whole creation as embodied in the Christ. That is, both the letter and the gospel understand the Christ as having a body that encompasses the cosmos. He does not have a body with spatial limits. This, of course, is in tension with the appearance of the Christ to Thomas to show him the scars of the nails in his hands and side. But this scene, obviously, reflects a later need to combat docetism. It also helps to understand the notion that the Risen

Lord occupies the whole universe, the cosmos. The physical body shown to the disciples is the temple. In antiquity, temples are the miniature material representations of the cosmic reality.

Both the letter *To the Colossians* and the gospel *According to John* draw significant conclusions from the understanding of the Living Christ as the *Pleroma*. The letter sees the crucifixion as the circumcision that makes the body of the *Pleroma* perfect (Col. 2:11). Baptized Christians are, therefore, "perfectly full in him" (Col. 2:10). The gospel, for its part, considers the *Pleroma* the source of the "grace upon grace" that Christians have received (1:16). The grace that keeps flowing is what incorporates Christians into the cosmic Fullness that is eternal life. The manifestation of the *Logos* "among us" was "full of grace and truth" (1:14). It is somewhat surprising that, while the prologue repeatedly confesses that God's grace has been manifested abundantly and effectively in the life of Jesus, the rest of the gospel does not refer again to Jesus as the *Logos* or to the grace received through him.

The *Logos* who was with God and was God (1:1) became flesh (1:14). This almost incomprehensible event is seen from two perspectives. First, the *Logos* "dwelt among us" in the flesh. We have noted that in the letter *To the Colossians* the bodily dwelling of the *Pleroma* in the Christ is described as a *katoikein*, as the establishment of a house with foundations reaching down. *According to John* normally uses the verb to abide (*menein*), with its rich semantic connotations. The dwelling of believers in the Son and the dwelling of the Father and the Son in the believers is described as an *abiding*. It is also said that the Father has many "abodes" where the believers will dwell (14:3). The case of the dwelling of the *Logos* in the flesh, however, is an encampment (*skenoein*), as the setting up of a tent by nomads in the desert. Thus, while according to the gospel the dwelling of the *Logos* in the flesh was temporary, according to the letter the bodily dwelling of the *Pleroma* in the Risen Christ is permanent.

In the few verses of the prologue the Johannine community also makes two most significant confessions, besides the ones already noted. First, "we have beheld his glory, glory as of the only Son from the Father" (1:14), and, second, "from his *Pleroma* we have all received grace upon grace" (1:16).

The first confession sets a contrast with Moses' desire to see the glory of God and God's unwillingness to comply. This is further indicated by the affirmation that "no one has ever seen God" but the Son "has made him known" (1:18). When Yahve asked Moses to leave Sinai and take the people to the promised land, Yahve assured Moses that his Presence would go with him and the people. To make sure that he was not imagining things but was actually being instructed by Yahve, Moses asked God to show him his glory. Yahve answered that he would show Moses his goodness and reveal to him his name, but he would not show Moses his face "for man shall not see me and live" (Ex. 33:20). Then Yahve told Moses how he would assure him that he was actually being instructed by Yahve (Ex. 33:21 – 23).

No doubt, when the Johannine community confesses "we beheld his glory," they are claiming for themselves a privilege Moses, the most revered personality in Judaism, did not enjoy. But they state their claim very carefully. They do not say that they saw the glory of Yahve. It is still true that "no one has ever seen God." They have seen the glory of the *Logos* who became flesh, and they can, therefore, give testimony of what it looked like. It was "as" the glory of the only Son from the Father that they saw the glory of God. In other words, they saw the glory given by the Father to the Son when he was glorified on the cross. Sinai may have been the place where God's goodness and name were revealed, but it was at the cross where the incarnate *Logos* was glorified, that the glory of God was revealed "as" the glory of the Son. During his encampment among humans the Son did not just reveal hypostases of God, God's goodness, or name, or mercy. Human beings got to know God and see God's glory. The Son revealed it to them. He was grace and truth incarnate. This is certainly a daring claim, even if nicely nuanced.

The second claim is no less daring: "From his *Pleroma* we have all received grace upon grace." While the first claim has its context in the Scriptures, the second fits within the Hellenistic religious and philosophical world, as we have already noticed. To have received grace upon grace from the *Pleroma* is to claim to be benefiting from the cosmic Christ in whom all things in the universe are pleased to have found a permanent home. As such, they claim to be living in the creation established by the Christ who has been glorified by the Father. It is on this basis that the members of the Johannine community claim to have eternal life and to be worshipping in the temple of his body (2:21) in spirit and in truth (4:24). To have received grace upon grace from the *Pleroma* is to live in the cosmos graced by creation and reconciliation. Those who make this confession lack nothing. They are perfectly full and at home in the cosmic Christ. This claim gave the Johannine community the courage to persist in a stance that set it at odds with emergent Rabbinic Pharisaism, and made it the object of distrust by some other Christians.

6

TO BEAR WITNESS TO THE TRUTH

More than any other biblical book, *According to John* is concerned with the necessity to distinguish truth from falsehood, what is true from what is spurious. It insists that it is of the essence to recognize The Truth. The narration of the life of Jesus among humans distinguishes what is true from what is not. Concern for truth naturally is taken today to be a concern for having information that is accurate. In this gospel, however, the concern is not for what is accurate, but for what is authentic. It is not for reliable information, but for genuine identity. Truth is not the essence which all true statements share. It is the essence of the life of God.

At the very beginning the narrator identifies the *Logos* as "the true light" (1:9). This could be a reference to the divine light that shone on the first three days "in the beginning." The sun that was created on the fourth day to facilitate the counting of the days, the months and the years, surely does not provide this kind of light. The true light is not that of the sun or the moon. It is God's light, the one the *Logos* creator of all things produced by *fiat* "in the beginning." The text, however, says even more. He not only produced it, but he *is* "the true light." To describe the incarnate *Logos* as light is analogical language. The light and Jesus are comparable because both illumine the road to be followed. But Jesus is the "true" light because the road he illumines is the one that ascends to the Father.

In the desert, during the Exodus, the Israelites ate manna, bread from heaven. But manna was bread "that perishes" (6:27,

49), bread of the world below, bread that could not be kept from one day to the next. Manna was bread to nourish life in the flesh. The true bread that descended from heaven, the one that nourishes eternal life, is not the bread Moses gave to the people in the desert. The Father gives "the true bread from heaven" (6:32). As a miracle that saves a people in crisis, the descent of manna does not compare with the descent of the Son of man. Here we are again reading analogical language. Manna and the Son descended to nourish life. But while one belonged to the world below and provided strength for life in the flesh, the other provides strength for life in the spirit, and only the world of the spirit is true. The Son is bread whose words "are spirit and life" (6:63). That is the difference between what Moses gave and what the Father sent. He who eats "true food [indeed]" and drinks "true drink [indeed]" has "life in him" and "abides in me, and I in him" (6:53 – 56).

Calling his disciples, Jesus singles out Nathanael, whose name means "Given by God," as the "[true] Israelite, indeed, in whom is no guile" (1:47). Of course, for "the Jews," the true Israelite is Jacob, the father of the twelve patriarchs of the tribes of Israel, for he is the one who wrestled with the angel of the Lord and won, and whose name ceased to be Jacob and became Israel (Gen. 32:27 – 28).

Jesus bypasses Jacob and gives this distinction to the one "Given by God." Jacob deceived his father, was deceived by his father-in-law, and recognized the stone that one night became his pillow as an earthly door to heaven. Nathanael, the true Israelite, the one without deceptions, would see the confirmation of Jesus as the Son of man who is the road to the Father. Jesus promises him that he will see the angels ascending and descending upon the Son of man (1:51). His vision is not to be compared to that of angels on a ladder (Gen. 28:12).

Just as there are many Israelites, but not all of them are true, there are also disciples who, like Jacob, are full of guile. The true disciples are those who "continue in my word" (8:31). This is a definition peculiar to *According to John*. What counts is not to have met, felt impressed by, or held a conversation with Jesus, or even to have left behind one's life work in order to go with Jesus. It is necessary to continue in his word. In this gospel, "to continue," "to abide" (*menein*) is a technical term. The one who "continues," who "remains," who "abides" in the One who *is* the Word (*Logos*), this one is the true disciple. Such a disciple recognizes that Jesus is not merely one more human being in a world where historical accidents cause the lives of human beings to turn out differently from the way they expected. No. His testimony, his word, is "true" because he knows from whence he came and where he is going (8:14). The true disciple is the one who abides in the reality of the One Sent by the Father, the only one who has ascended to heaven. That is The Truth.

It is not a question of being convinced of the truth of some dogmatic declaration. Rather, it is about the person of Jesus who, walking the dusty roads of Palestine, did not seem to be more than the son of a carpenter from Nazareth. This person claims to be the One Sent by the Father who will return to where he came from. Where he is going, he says, no one on their own can go. That is the Word in which his true disciples "abide."

On the contrary, of Satan it is said that "he was a murderer from the beginning, and has nothing to do with the truth, because there is no truth in him. When he lies, he speaks according to his own nature, for he is a liar and the father of lies" (8:44). This description is the setup for the punch line in the vitriolic polemic Johannine Christians are having with "the Jews." After "the Jews" accuse Jesus of being a bastard (8:41), Jesus accuses "the Jews" of having Satan, the father of lies, as their father. Thus the contrast between Jesus, the Truth, and Satan, the Lie, is given ultimate shape. It says it all.

Jesus is the truth and speaks the truth because of his relation with the Father, whose being is ultimate truth. As Jesus says, "He who sent me is true" (7:28). The One Sent is true because he does not seek his own glory, but that of the one who sent him (7:18). Thus he tells the truth (8:45) and his judgment is true, because in effect it is the judgment of the one who sent him (8:16).

The prologue makes a plain distinction: "The law was given through Moses; grace and truth came through Jesus Christ" (1:17). Truth is a reality that does not belong to the world below. It is not an object in the same way in which the law is. Truth cannot be "given." It can only be seen, experienced, lived. Truth is a reality of the spirit, and like the spirit cannot be given "by measure" (3:34). The spirit makes it possible for human beings "to be born from above" (3:3), to be "born … of God" (1:13), "to be born of the spirit" (3:8). He who is thusly born receives the testimony of him "who comes from above [and] is above all" (3:31). On that basis he "sets his seal," that is, swears 'with his right hand on the Bible' "that God is true" (3:31 – 32). No human being may be credited with a more transcendent affirmation.

To those born from above God has given a special revelation. What they receive, however, is not a new law or a new doctrine. They receive the opportunity to experience "grace and truth" as manifested in the person of Jesus. He is "the way, and the truth, and the life" (14:6). He is the way of life for those who have access to the realm of truth. The truth revealed in him is the life lived by those born of the spirit. Revealing his mission, he said "I came that they may have life, and have it abundantly" (10:10). The true disciples who continue in his word are not the ones who are doctrinal experts and give sound theological pronouncements, but the ones who abide in the life that was revealed by the Father in the person of the Son. As Jesus says: "If any man's will is to do his will, he shall know whether the teaching is from God, or whether I am speaking on my own authority" (7:17). In other words, the evaluation of Jesus' claim to be the true life cannot be done on the basis of purely intellectual judgments. His claim is taken seriously only by those who have the will to do God's will. A life that carries out God's will is the prerequisite. Understanding the validity of Jesus' claim is not a pure act of the mind; it involves the will. This combination of will and intellect is the substance of faith, and what it apprehends is not information but true life.

Such a disciple does not wander in the darkness of the world. He has no need to hide his doings for fear of being found out because his works are evil. "He who does what is true [the truth] comes to the light" (3:21). The truth is not something to be stored in the mind. The truth is to be done, to be actualized, to be lived by those who "abide" in the One who is "the light of the world" (8:12).

Before Pilate, who foolishly brags about his power of life and death over him, Jesus reveals again the purpose of his presence on earth in these words: "I have come into the world to bear witness to the truth" (18:37). He witnesses to life in the Spirit, that is true, eternal life. He witnesses to the life of God who is Spirit (4:24). Hearing this pronouncement, Pilate can only shake his head, make a grandiose gesture with his arms in the air and, frustrated, ask, "What is truth?" (18:38).

For those who are from below and can speak only about earthly things (3:31), it is impossible to know what is truth. Only those who have received "the gift of God" know what truth is. They have drunk the "living water" that transforms them into "springs of water welling up to eternal life" (4:10, 14) and have eaten of "the bread of God ... which comes down from heaven, and gives life to the world" (6:33).

Only those who have ceased being slaves and have been set free by the Son (8:35 – 36) receive the testimony to the truth that the Son, as the One Sent by the Father, makes effective. They are the ones who continue in his word and know the truth. As a consequence the truth makes them free (8:31 - 32). The truth does not set them free from falsehoods. Knowing the truth is to have an intimate relation with it, not to grasp it intellectually. The truth makes true disciples free from death. The "spirit of truth" (14:17; 15:26; 16:13) then causes the testimony of the Son to remain (*menein*) in his disciples. The truth that sets slaves free from sin and death is the eternal life to which the Son came to bear witness. In *According to John*, Son, truth and life are one and the same thing.

The way in which *According to John* deals with truth does not, of course, envision philosophical concerns with truth as non-contradition or as universals that exist apart or at least distinct from all its instances. Neither does it concern itself with the modern quest of what is understood as "factual" truth. Scientists are concerned with the ways in which nature works; their interest is to know the truth about nature. Historians seek to establish what actually happened in the past; their interest is to establish what is historically true, the facts about history. These modern scientific and historical concerns were not within the intellectual horizon of the early Christians.

The Johannine community is aware of the Platonic doctrine that truth is not to be found in the material world. To this understanding it provided two correctives. On the one hand, it did not identify the truth with the Platonic forms or ideas which place truth in the realm of the intellect. The truth, it proclaimed, is in the being of God that was revealed in the life of the Son among human beings (1:18). On the other hand, the material world is not a flawed creation done by an incompetent divine agent. It is the direct creation of the *Logos* who is God; He dwelt in the material world to infuse it with eternal life.

Scientific and historical truths are bound to the evidence available to sustain them, and because of their dependence on it are bound to change as new evidence becomes available. Religious truth, of necessity, transcends the evidence to dwell in the realm of the Spirit. To transcend the evidence, however, is not to negate it. To affirm the realm where the Spirit works is to affirm that the Lord who is Spirit (4:24) is also the God of creation. The scientific study of nature and the past on the basis of the evidence is a legitimate human endeavor that makes life in the world more meaningful and pleasant. There can be no contradictions between the scientific and historical evidence and what is proclaimed as the Truth of the Gospel. Even as religious truth transcends the material world to affirm the world of the Spirit, it also finds in the material world the analogies with which to illumine the Truth of the Spirit.

In his conversation with the Samaritan woman Jesus makes the point that the Father seeks "true worshippers" who "worship in spirit and in truth" (4:24), rather than in temples set up on mountains. The worship of the Father, of necessity transcends the limitations of the material world. For those who worship the Father truth is found in the life of the Father and the Son, in the world of the Spirit. The Truth of the Gospel belongs to the realm of the Spirit, and it is to that realm that Jesus was a witness. Because of his witness human beings may be believers who live and worship in Spirit and in truth.

7
Who Is this Son of Man?

It has long been recognized that the various titles given to Jesus were assigned as a conscious effort to give him recognizable identity. The titles were culled from the Scriptures, and had acquired already distinctive status in the religious discourse of the time. As we have had opportunity to notice, attributes or faculties of God had achieved semi-individualized personality and were considered divine agents who accomplished specific tasks on earth. This was the case with the *glory*, the *spirit*, the *name*, the *wisdom*, the *word* and the *face* of God, to name the most notable.

In *According to John* the *word*, the *spirit* and the *glory* are major protagonists in the drama of the gospel. The Scriptures had also set up expectations about distinctive personages who would fulfill important functions in the future of Israel. Most prominent among them were the Messiah, the Prophet like Moses, and the Suffering Servant. *According to John* refers to the Messiah and the Prophet. It does not allude to the Suffering Servant since its Christology does not include the role played by this figure. References to the Messiah and the Prophet, however, seem at times to be ambiguous, apparently because the Johannine community understands the role of Jesus differently from the ones commonly assigned to these eschatological figures. Something similar seems also to be the case with the title King and the expectations it aroused in the hearts of the Jews.

The account of the gathering of Jesus' first disciples says that Philip found Nathanael and told him, "We have found him of whom Moses in the law and also the prophets wrote, Jesus of Nazareth, the son of Joseph" (1:45). This initial identification is also the one current among "the Jews" (6:42). When the soldiers guided by Judas come to the garden on the other side of the Kidron valley and are asked by Jesus, "Whom do you seek?" they identify the one they are looking for as "Jesus of Nazareth." This identification, however, is quite inadequate. In typical Johannine style, the question of Nathanael in response to Philip's information turns out to be rhetorical: "Can anything good come out of Nazareth?" The obvious answer is of course, no. But, the reality is that both Philip and Nathanael must come to understand that Jesus is not from Nazareth. He is the One Sent by the Father from above (8:23). "The Jews," and the soldiers who looked for him at the garden, never understood this.

Besides, frequently throughout the gospel Jesus is identified as "this man" (6:52; 7:31, 35; 10:4; 18:17, 29, 30; 19:12, 21). This view of Jesus of Nazareth finds its apotheosis at his trial. To "the Jews" who are insisting on his crucifixion, Pilate presents Jesus with the words, "Behold the man" (19:7). In the world below, the world ruled by the Roman empire, Jesus is from Nazareth and just another man, "this man." To know Jesus as a man from Nazareth, the son of Joseph, or this man, is not to know him at all.

When he actually met Jesus, Nathanael proclaimed "You are the Son of God! You are the King of Israel!" (1:49). Certainly, Son of God and King of Israel are some steps up the ladder from "this man," or Jesus of Nazareth. Nathanael has been able to see something special about Jesus; the titles he assigns to Jesus are synonymous. In antiquity the king was a son of God. He was the anointed of the Lord. It is not likely, however, that the gospel wishes its readers to accept these titles as sufficient. On the two occasions in which the people intended to make him king, Jesus disapproves of their efforts. When after the feeding of the multitude the crowd tried to make him king by force, Jesus escaped to a mountain alone

(6:15). When after the raising of Lazarus the crowd proclaimed him King of Israel, Jesus "found a young ass and sat upon it." The narrator then explains that later the disciples found a Scriptural text with which to give new meaning to the event, but at first they had not understood Jesus' disapproval of the reaction of the crowd (12:12 – 18). In *According to John*, the entry to the city with the crowd proclaiming him king does not culminate with the king taking possession of the temple, and "the Jews" deciding on that account to kill him, as in the synoptic gospels. In this gospel the decision of "the Jews" to kill him was taken quite a few days before as a consequence of his raising Lazarus from the dead (11:53). The crowd's demonstration in favor of Jesus' becoming their king only serves to confirm among "the Jews" the wisdom of their previous decision (12:19).

At the trial and the crucifixion the title *king* is given a new twist. Pilate presents Jesus to the crowd as "King of the Jews" (rather than King of Israel). Like Nathanael, who had originally seen Jesus as a man from Nazareth and later proclaimed him King of Israel, Pilate, who had said to the crowd "Behold the man," later presents him saying: "Behold, your king" (19:14). On both occasions he is demonstrating his ignorance. Then, when "the Jews" choose Barabbas as the beneficiary of a Passover pardon, Pilate asks: "Shall I crucify your king?" "The Jews," who deny that Jesus is their king, again with typical Johannine irony declare themselves apostates whose only king is Caesar (19:15). Pilate insists on Jesus' status as king and has a title placed on his cross written in Hebrew, Latin and Greek: "Jesus of Nazareth, King of the Jews" (19:19). Here the original identification by Philip and the last by Pilate have been conflated. As far as Rome is concerned, it has executed a seditious impostor. Whether or not they are considered sons of God, kings are men with political power in a world where power is highly contested. To know Jesus as the King of the Jews is not to know him at all.

In *According to John* the title Christ is also problematic. It is curious to find this title for the first time on the lips of John the

Baptist. Twice he thinks it necessary to make sure everyone understands that he is not the Christ (1:20; 3:28). Of course, this kind of protestation only raises suspicions. The gospel explicitly states that the disciples of John the Baptist expressed their displeasure that Jesus was siphoning John's audience. The ministry of John the Baptist, undoubtedly, had a messianic aura in the eyes of the people. That is the only explanation for the fact that Herod feared him and decapitated him. The ministry of Jesus also had a messianic aura, and that is why the Roman procurator crucified him. Messianic roles had originally only political implications. Eventually they acquired also religious ones. Thus, the Dead Sea Scrolls refer to both a priestly and a royal Messiah.

It is interesting that in his conversation with the Samaritan woman, when Jesus tells her that she had had five husbands and was now living with a man who was not her husband, she says: "Sir, I perceive that you are a prophet" (4:19). When Jesus tells her that there will come a time when true worship will not be carried out in temples, the woman says: "I know that Messiah is coming (he who is called the Christ)." Then Jesus says to her: "I who speak to you am he" (4:26). This response of his is similar to the one he gave the soldiers who came to the garden looking for Jesus of Nazareth. The woman, however, does not trust Jesus' claim. She goes into town to report Jesus' presence at the well and says to the town people that the stranger had told her "all that I ever did." Then she asks "Can this be the Christ?" (4:29). She is only guessing. It is noteworthy that after the people of Sychar had Jesus with them for two days they did not come to the conclusion that the woman's suspicion was correct. Rather than declaring Jesus the Christ, they proclaimed him "Savior of the world" (4:42). The Christ, instead, is only a Savior of Israel. In this episode the move is from prophet to Christ to Savior of the world. The Samaritans have moved up the ladder farther than Nathanael.

Something similar happens with "the Jews." Frustrated they ask Jesus: "If you are the Christ tell us plainly" (10:24). Instead of answering plainly, as he had to the Samaritan woman, Jesus faults their lack of faith by explaining that they "do not belong to my sheep" (10:26). In other words, Jesus avoids being identified as the Christ. The concern of "the Jews" with the Messiah (Christ) is not one that Jesus is eager to clarify. Pursuing the question of a messianic role is going down the wrong alley. As far as "the Jews" are concerned, of course, Jesus does not fit their expectations about the Christ. According to them the law indicates that the Christ remains forever, but Jesus is talking about his departure (12:34). Besides, the Christ is a descendant of David who comes from Bethlehem, the city of David, but Jesus is from Galilee (7:41 – 42).

The most direct affirmation of Jesus as the Christ is the confession of Martha: "I believe that you are the Christ, the Son of God, he who is coming into the world" (11:27). In this case the synonym to Son of God is Christ rather than King, as in the case of Nathanael's confession. But Martha adds the explanation, "he who is coming into the world" — the one we have been expecting is now coming. In the dialogue between Martha and Jesus that precedes her confession we learn that she is working with traditional apocalyptic expectations, and that Jesus corrects her by pointing out that what she expects from the future is already here: "I am the resurrection and the life" (11:25). Martha's confession that he is the Christ, "he who is coming into the world" appeals to a present act of God sending the one being expected. Jesus does give as the definition of eternal life "that they know thee the only true God, and Jesus Christ whom thou hast sent" (17:3). In a way, Martha's confession of Jesus as the Christ may be the Johannine equivalent of Peter's confession of Jesus as the Christ in *According to Mark* (Mk. 8:29). In the case of Peter's confession, Jesus responds by redefining the meaning of the title. The Christ is not the anointed King who rules on a throne. The Christ must suffer, be reviled, be mocked, be spat upon, be scourged and be killed (Mk. 8:31; 9:31; 10:33 – 34). Martha's confession is left alone.

Most frequently Jesus refers to himself as the Son who is close to and has been sent by the Father. The Father, in turn, is described as the One Who Sent the Son into the world. The closeness of the

Father and the Son is evident since he who has seen the Son "has seen the Father" (14:9); as Jesus says, "the Father is in me, and I am in the Father" (10:38). In his most daring claim Jesus says: "I and the Father are one" (10:30).

It is puzzling that when Jesus said "The Father is working still, and I am working" (5:17), "the Jews" understood that he was "making himself equal with God" (5:18) and, from what follows, it is clear that Jesus agrees with them. But after he makes the claim "I and the Father are one," and "the Jews" are about to stone him, Jesus asks them "for which of these [works] do you stone me?" (10:32). They then explain that they are not going to stone him for what he did but for what he said. They are going to stone him for blaspheming, "because you, being a man, make yourself God" (10:33). Rather than agreeing with them, this time Jesus retorts: "Do you say of him whom the Father consecrated and sent into the world, 'You are blaspheming,' because I said, 'I am the Son of God'?" (10:36).

Jesus' defense is based on a passage that is credited to "your law" (that of "the Jews"), but is actually a quote from Psalm 82, not the Pentateuch. The Psalm is an appeal for God to sit in judgment at the "divine council" and correct the injustices performed by the gods in the council. They are being partial to the wicked. God instructs them that, instead, they should have been dealing fairly with "the weak and the fatherless … the afflicted and the destitute." They should have been rescuing them from the hand of the wicked. Because of their perversion of justice, God tells them: "You are gods, sons of the Most High, all of you, nevertheless you shall die like men" (Ps. 82:6 – 7). The Psalm gives the rationale for the miscarriages of justice taking place among humans and God's solution to this problem. But the Psalm also makes use of the mythological imagery of a polytheistic past in which Yahve is the head of the heavenly pantheon. As such, God is punishing the gods by condemning them to die like men on account of their miscarriages of justice. By the first century CE, however, Judaism had become thoroughly monotheistic, and the Psalm is being interpreted to say that God is addressing Jews, those "to whom the word of God came" (10:35), rather than the gods of the Pantheon. It would seem that the Johannine community is appealing to the Psalm to say that humans are called gods in Scripture.

The story assumes that the audience knows the Psalm by heart and would supply the identification of the gods as sons of the Most High. On the basis of this tendentious interpretation, Jesus' argument is that since all Jews are called gods, sons of the Most High, he should not be considered a blasphemer for claiming to be the Son of God. How his claim to be one with the Father has become the claim that he is the Son of God is left unexplained. This is the ambiguity that we noticed when the title Son of God is attached to the title Christ, or King. Certainly the claim is not that, as a Son of God, Jesus is like all Jews which, according to their way of reading the Psalm, are designated in "their law" as sons of God. As happened with the title Christ, the title Son of God is used in reference to human beings.

Central to all four gospels is the designation of Jesus as the Son of man. Not too long ago it was common to say that Son of God called attention to the divine nature of Jesus, and Son of man to his human nature. Such a view is based on an anachronism and is totally disallowed by the evidence, which rather indicates the contrary – that Son of God is actually a title given to human beings, while Son of man is a title for a divine being. The understanding of Jesus in terms of a human and a divine nature did not enter Christian theology until the fifth century CE. As we have been noticing, Son of God is a title that fits humans, like the Messiah or the king. Son of man, on the other hand, is definitely a designation for a divine being.

The title has its roots in the Danielic vision of one "like a Son of man" who receives the power that has been taken away from the little horn that had taken down three horns from the beast with ten horns. One "like a Son of man" comes in the clouds of heaven and is presented to the Ancient of Days. From him the Son of man receives everlasting dominion (Dan. 7:7 – 14). This apocalyptic figure became the personification of the final vindication of the justice of God on earth that puts an end to the injustices suffered by the weak and defenseless people of God who live under the rule of princes who disregard the will of God.

The Son of man plays a prominent role in the apocalyptic scenarios of the synoptic gospels. At the Parousia the Son of man comes on the clouds of heaven as the judge who establishes justice on earth. In these gospels the title is expanded to include other functions. Besides being the one who manifests himself in a glorious future appearance in the clouds, the Son of man is also the one who must suffer at the hands of men before he is vindicated at his resurrection (Mk. 8:31; 9:31; 10:33). Speaking about himself in the third person as the Son of man, Jesus has the authority to exercise divine prerogatives. The Son of man can forgive sins (Mk. 2:11) and is the Lord of the Sabbath (Mk. 2:28).

Just as *According to John* turns on its head the messianic secret motif central to the synoptic gospels, as we noticed in a previous meditation, it also re-designs the portrait of the Son of man. Rather than being the one who will return to earth on the clouds of heaven in a glorious future and end all the world's injustices, the Son of man is the one who must be "lifted up" as Moses lifted up the serpent in the desert (3:13 - 14; 6:62; 8:28; 12:34; 13:31). Instead of appearing in glory with myriads of angels in an apocalyptic denouement, the Son of man is glorified by being "lifted up" on a cross (12:23).

The synoptic gospels insist on the necessity for the Son of man to suffer at the hands of men, be reviled and mocked before being raised after three days (Mk. 3:31; 9:31; 10:32). In *According to John* what is necessary is for men and women to eat the flesh of the Son of man in order to live (6:27, 53). Of course, in the Johannine vocabulary to eat is to believe. It is necessary to believe in the Son of man in order to see and live (9:35 – 37). The Son of Man is the one who gives out "the food that endures (abides) to eternal life." He can do this because "on him has God the Father set his seal" (6:27). While he who believes in the testimony of Jesus "set his seal to this, that God is true" (3:33), God the Father "has set his seal" that the Son of Man provides eternal life. This explanation gives to the Son of Man a most privileged role as the one who personifies the accomplishment of Jesus' mission.

Finally, and a bit closer to the picture found in the synoptics, the Son of man is the one who judges (5:27). But, again, the judgment of the Son of man is taking place right now as people react to the presence of the One Sent by the Father among them (9:39). To the man born blind, after he gave him sight, Jesus asks: "Do you believe in the Son of man?" (9:35). The poor man admits ignorance. He would like to know who the Son of man is so as to believe in him. Jesus then informs him, "You have seen him. It is he who speaks to you" (9:37). The situation is similar to that of the soldiers at the garden who were looking for Jesus of Nazareth and that of the Samaritan woman who knew about a coming Messiah. In this case, when Jesus identifies himself as the Son of man the ex-blind man responds by saying "I believe" and worshipping Jesus. This is the title that elicits justified worship. By contrast, "the Jews" are left wondering "Who is this Son of man?" (12:34).

At the beginning of the gospel Jesus gave a promise to Nathanael, who had proclaimed him Son of God and King of Israel: "Truly, truly, I say to you, you will see heaven open, and the angels of God ascending and descending upon the Son of man" (1:51). Here the vision of Jacob and the vision of Daniel have been juxtaposed in a most creative way to provide a clue to the reader of the gospel. The heavens will not open for the Son of man to descend on the clouds of heaven. The heavens will open for the angels to ascend and descend upon the Son of man. He is the ladder on which the believer has access to the Father. Jacob who had a vision, believed, and worshipped, building an altar upon the stone that had served him as a pillow. The promise given to Nathanael is also given to readers of this gospel, promising them that they will also see the heavens open and the way to the Father revealed to them so that they too may believe and worship. As the one who must be lifted up, the Son of man is the one who overcomes the chasm that separates the flesh from the Spirit. When the heavens are open and angels travel between the world above and the world below it is possible for those living in the flesh to see the Father in the One Sent and to worship him. It is only when they recognize the Son of man in Jesus that human beings have identified him correctly.

8

The Hour Is Coming, and Now Is

The gospel *According to John* invites us to enter an environment quite different from the better-known one found in the synoptic gospels. In these gospels Jesus preaches about the kingdom of God by means of parables that describe activities and objects of everyday village life. In *According to John*, as we have already pointed out in previous meditations, Jesus preaches himself as the One Sent by the Father. His message is "I Am." In the synoptics the ministry of Jesus takes place in Galilee, and he is in Jerusalem only for the last week of his life. In *According to John* his ministry takes place mostly in Jerusalem. In all four gospels Jesus refers to the saying, "A prophet is not without honor except in his own country." But while the land in which Jesus is without honor in the synoptics is Galilee (Mk. 6:4), in *According to John* it is Jerusalem (4:44).

In the synoptics, Jesus' audacity in expelling the money changers and the sellers of animals from the temple provoked the authorities' decision to kill him. Such a demonstration of power in the cosmic universe of the temple could not be tolerated. It was a public challenge that the authorities confronted decisively. In *According to John* the account of the expulsion of the money changers and the sellers of animals suggests an event of greater violence than the one described in the synoptics. Here Jesus holds in his hand a whip and throws them out as if he were herding cattle. But the event is framed by the provision of the best wine at the wedding feast at Cana and the conversation with Nicodemus, the gentleman of the night. The demonstration of power at the temple takes place on a Passover two or three years before his passion and has nothing to do with the decision to kill him. In this gospel the officers of the temple and the Pharisees decide to kill Jesus because the resurrection of Lazarus is causing the people to give too much authority to him (11:48).

In the synoptic gospels Jesus pronounces apocalyptic discourses that predict the future signs and the characteristics of the times just before the coming of the Son of Man in glory. In *According to John* there are no apocalyptic discourses. The present already contains what apocalypticists expect in the future.

One of the best known images in apocalypticism is "the harvest." In the sypnoptics Jesus tells several parables that demonstrate the need to have the patience and the hope of the farmers who must wait until the harvest in order to see the fruit of their labors. The parables also illustrate how the harvest reveals the quality of the soil, the need to separate that which was sown from the weeds, or the internal power at work in seeds.

In *According to John* there are only two parables from nature: "the wind blows where it wills, and you hear the sound of it, but you do not know whence it comes or whither it goes" (3:8), and "unless a grain of wheat falls into the earth and dies, it remains alone; but if it dies, it bears much fruit" (12:24). One illustrates that those born "from above" don't know how it happened, and the other explains that for life to bear fruit a death must intervene. Neither one has to do with the kingdom of God and the future. Both illustrate the present.

In general, Jesus disconnects what happens in nature from what happens in history. To the disciples who worry about getting something to eat at lunch time (the sixth hour), Jesus says, "my food is to do the will of him who sent me, and to accomplish his work. Do you not say, 'There are yet four months, then comes the harvest'? I tell you, lift up your eyes, and see how the fields are already white for harvest. He who reaps receives wages, and gathers fruit for eternal life, so that sower and reaper may rejoice together" (4:34 – 36). In the case of the harvest for eternal life there is no need to wait four months to harvest the fruit. In this case the sowers and the reapers rejoice together. The present is witnessing both the sowing and the reaping.

The food provided by nature for the sustenance of the flesh depends on processes that require time. The food of Jesus, to do the will of his Father and to accomplish his work, is effective at once. The work of Jesus does not reach its completion at a future apocalyptic event. His work was accomplished, finished, on the cross. Very aware of this, before breathing his last, Jesus said: "It is finished" (19:30). Surely this word on the cross is the announcement that he had done the will of his Father and fully accomplished his work. With this word the future is disarmed. By his descent and his ascent the Son of man made possible eternal life. The more abundant life is already a reality among human beings. The seed of eternal life is now multiplying and bearing fruit.

The earthly life of the Son of man took place according to a set schedule. It did not accommodate itself to capricious circumstances that just happened. His life followed the outline established even "before the foundation of the world" (17:5, 24). On more than one occasion what seemed inevitable did not happen because "his hour had not yet come" (7:5, 30; 8:20). There were times when it looked like the animosity of those opposed to him had reached a breaking point. Their anger was going to become violent with predictable results. What seemed unavoidable, however, did not occur. It was not his time yet. For others, however, for example his brothers, their "time is always here" (7:6).

The hour of Jesus, no doubt, arrives at its appointed time, and Jesus knows how to face it. Already in Jerusalem for the Passover, Jesus announces, "The hour has come for the Son of man to be glorified" (12:23). The narrator later tells us that a few days before the feast, since he "knew that his hour had come" (13:1), Jesus began to wash the disciples' feet. This was an act of solidarity before death that levels the master and his servants. Jesus did it as an example that his disciples should imitate. Then he identified Judas and told him, "What you are going to do, do quickly" (13:27). Since the hour was already fixed, and Jesus was doing what was necessary to be on time, having done what he needed to do for his disciples before the hour arrived, he orders Judas to act quickly. He is in control, orchestrating what is happening.

Since the disciples are expected to identify themselves with their master, it is not surprising that one day their hour will also arrive. Thus, Jesus warns them: "the hour is coming when whoever kills you will think he is offering service to God.... But I have said these things to you, that when their hour comes you may remember that I told you of them" (16:2, 4). Again, as the one who knows not only what his mission is and how it will be accomplished, but also knows what is the role of his disciples in the world, Jesus warns them about their hour. They also now exist for a definite purpose. The shift from the second to the third person plural in the text is one of the many perplexities found in it. It is best understood by recognizing that the narrator is having Jesus predict the expulsion of his disciples from the synagogue knowing that those who experience the expulsion were not the contemporaries of Jesus. On that account Jesus refers to those being persecuted as "them" rather than "you."

What is, then, the significance of the hour that marks the life of Jesus and that of his disciples? We may find a clue about this in Jesus' explanation that the sorrow the disciples would experience as witnesses to his crucifixion would turn into joy when they see him alive afterwards. "When a woman is in travail she has sorrow, because her hour has come; but she no longer remembers the anguish, for joy that a child is born into the world" (16:21). Analogies usually make one point and break down. The analogy of the woman giving birth to a child actually has two points of comparison. Both Jesus at his crucifixion and the woman at childbirth are at their hour. Both the disciples and the woman giving birth experience anguish and pain that ends in joy. The analogy may also be stretched to make a third comparison. At her hour the woman gives birth to a child. At his hour on the cross, lifted up, Jesus gives birth to all those who believe in him and are born from above. At the same time, because his body has become a new temple (2:21), representative of a new creation, those born from above now live in the creation of the world of the Spirit and Truth, where worship is unmediated communion with God. The hour of death is the hour that produces much fruit.

It may also be noted that this analogy reflects the limited view of womanhood prevalent at that time. According to popular opinion women existed to bring children to the world. The "hour" of the woman is the hour of giving birth to "a man" (*anthropos*). Clearly, "the hour" is when a person's reason for living is revealed—when one's purpose is exposed. When certain Greeks who have come to Jerusalem to worship at Passover ask Philip: "Sir, we would see Jesus," Philip does not know what to do with this request and consults with Andrew. Then both present the request to Jesus. The reaction of Jesus is: "Now is my soul troubled. And what shall I say? 'Father, save me from this hour'? No, for this purpose I have come to this hour" (12:27).

The scene with the Greeks is the Johannine equivalent to the scene in the garden of Gethsemane in the synoptics, but it does not describe agony and supplications. While it alludes to the personal importance of the moment, what it demonstrates is the resolute decision of the one who knows for what purpose he came to the world. The immediate response by Jesus to the request of the Greeks, "The hour has come for the Son of man to be glorified" (12:23), is definitively described by Jesus at the beginning of his farewell prayer: "Father, the hour has come; glorify thy Son" (17:1). The purpose for his being in the world had to be accomplished. Jesus was to be "lifted up" to where he had come from. The hour in which he was to account for the reason of his being in the world had come. The Father had to glorify him, crucify him. In this gospel authority over life and death comes only "from above" (19:11).

Three times we read "the hour is coming, and now is." These declarations are worthy of special attention. In these cases the reference is not to the life of Jesus. They have to do with specific experiences of Christians who are living after the glorification of the Son of man.

It is after his resurrection and after he has breathed the Holy Spirit on the disciples (20:22), that Christians can worship the Father in Spirit and in truth (4:23). "The hour is coming, and now is," when true worshippers, the type of worshippers the Father seeks, will adore effectively. This acceptable worship, performed in the temple which is the body of the Risen Christ, is now possible and marks the existence of Christians after the resurrection.

Likewise, it is after his resurrection that "the hour is coming, and now is" when "the dead" hear the voice of the Son of Man and those who hear it pass from death to life (5:25). Verse 28 then contrasts these "dead" with those who are in their tombs. It is now that the dead in their sins hear the voice of the Son, believe, and pass from death to life. Those dead in their sins need not wait till harvest time. Eternal life is already a reality among Christians.

This expression is also used specifically in reference to the identity and the vocation of the true disciples. "The hour is coming, indeed it has come, when you will be scattered" (16:32). As disciples of the One who came to bear witness to the truth, the hour of truth comes to all his followers. This is when they must be willing to be rejected by "the world" in the manner in which "the world" rejected him who came to save it. To all his disciples, from the point of view of *According to John*, "the hour is coming, and now is" because the lifting up of the Son of man has been effective and must be re-enacted in the lives of his disciples. They must now accomplish the purpose of their lives.

The Christian community shaped by these intensive theological reflections on the life and the death of Jesus as the incarnate *Logos* saw itself as the blessed beneficiary of the mission that the Son of man had carried to completion with total success. This conviction, however, did not cause its members to overflow with reprehensible pride or egotistical celebrations. On the contrary, it caused them to concentrate their attention on the need to love each other. It also caused them to institutionalize the washing of each others feet as a sign of solidarity with Christ when facing biological death; this was an institution ignored by the synoptic gospels. The transfer of the accomplishment of salvation from the future to the present means that the ultimate purpose of a Christian life is not to be revealed in a future life. The *eschaton*, the final, ultimate goal of life is to actualize communities of love where worship of the Father takes place in Spirit and in truth, that is to say, by life that is empowered by faith here on earth now. Rather than to promote rituals or ascetic practices, or promote escapes from the world in journeys to heaven now or at a final denouement, *According to John* invites believers to live a full life conscious that as those born from above they now live in fulfillment of their vocation as keepers of the word of Jesus.

9
ON THE THIRD DAY

One of the characteristics of the gospel *According to John* is that the main events in the life of Jesus are connected to Jewish feasts or specific times. The expulsion of the money changers and traders from the temple happened on a Passover (2:13). The feeding of the five thousand took place on another Passover (6:4). Apparently Jesus did not go up to Jerusalem for this one. The healing of the paralytic at the portals of the Pool of Bethesda in Jerusalem was done on "a feast of the Jews" (5:1). (Most readers of this gospel think this was also a Passover). All the gospels agree that Jesus died at Passover time (11:55).

On the basis of references to four Passovers in *According to John* (counting as a Passover the feast of chapter 5), it is said that the ministry of Jesus lasted three and a half years. The Passover references are thus taken for their chronological value. (According to the Synoptics the ministry of Jesus may have lasted less than a year). In this context it is well to remember that other events in *According to John* are given time references with deep reserves of meaning that transcend temporality. The alluded time serves to give the proper context in which to understand what is taking place.

For example, we read that the Feast of Tabernacles was approaching, and Jesus went up to Jerusalem incognito (7:2). This feast commemorates the providence of God during the desert wanderings at the Exodus. One of the most prominent miracles at that time had been the rock from which water came forth to satisfy the needs of the people in that parched land. The feast lasted seven days. At its culmination the priests descended from the temple to the spring of Siloam and then carried jars full of water up to the altar of sacrifices in the court of the Gentiles. The people followed them, also carrying jars full of water. As they came to the court of the Gentiles they would all pour the water in their jars on the altar, and the water would then run freely on the court. In this way the feast not only transformed the altar into the rock from which water flowed freely in the desert, but also announced the fulfillment of Ezekiel's prophecy that a river would flow from the temple on Zion and run east to sweeten and give life to the waters of the Dead Sea (Ez. 47:1 – 12).

According to John says: "On the last day of the feast, the great day, Jesus stood up and proclaimed, 'If any one thirst let him come to me, and drink he who believes in me. As the Scripture has said: "Out of his entrails shall flow rivers of living water""" (7:37 – 38, my translation). The narrator then tells the reader, "Now this he said about the Spirit, which those who believed in him were to receive; for as yet the Spirit had not been given, because Jesus was not yet glorified" (7:39). The reference to the Feast of Tabernacles gives us the clue to understand the words of Jesus. The water from the rock in the desert and the water of the river that gives life to the Dead Sea are not to be compared with the water of the Spirit (3:5; compare with 4:14) that flows from the body of the Glorified. No doubt the description of the soldier opening a wound with his spear in the side of Jesus on the cross, from which water and blood flowed (19:34), is meant to demonstrate the fulfillment of Jesus' words at the Feast of Tabernacles. This saying of Jesus would not be understandable if the reader had not been told that it was at the great day of the Feast of Tabernacles that this all happened.

Temporal references aim to give the reader the theological frame within which to understand what is being told. This is also the case in the reference to Passover in chapter six and the feeding of the five thousand. The discourse about the true bread which descended from heaven contrasts the miracle of manna with the bread of life provided by the Glorified. "It is the Spirit that gives life, the flesh is of no avail" (6:63). Again, a formative Exodus event provides the context for the saying of Jesus and brings out its significance.

Other episodes in *According to John* have temporal references with evident theological meaning. In a previous meditation I referred to the washing of the disciples' feet as an example the disciples were to imitate to confirm their solidarity with Christ. Jesus carried out this act when he "knew that his hour had come to depart out of this world .... Jesus knowing .... that he had come from God and was going to God" (13:1, 3). In other words, the washing of the disciples' feet must be understood in reference to his death, his departure out of this world, his return to God. In every case the temporal reference provides the key for understanding.

After having eaten the bread dipped in wine that Jesus gave him, Judas went out from the room in which Jesus and the disciples had supper. The disciples thought he was going to buy what was necessary to celebrate Passover the next day. The narrator, however, informs the reader that "it was night" (13:30). Having noticed the function of the other temporal references, we cannot fail to note that the reference to the night is not just noticing the time of day. In this gospel, as already seen, the contrast between day and night, darkness and light, is given theological significance. That Judas has departed from the company of Jesus into the darkness of night, and that his fellow disciples misinterpret his departure, only serves to set the tone for what is to follow.

Throughout the gospel there are references to Nicodemus, the one who came to Jesus "by night" (3:2; 7:50; 19:39). Jesus himself makes clear that "if any one walks in the night, he stumbles" (11:10). Worrying that the bodies of the three who had been crucified not be exposed to view on the Sabbath, "the Jews" asked Pilate to accelerate their death by breaking their legs. Once this was done, the victim was not able to lift his body by putting pressure on the nail that went through his feet. The full weight of his body hung from the arms and the lower thorax was more tensely stretched, making it very difficult for the diaphragm to pump air into the lungs. Those crucified then died from asphyxia or cardiac arrest.

Eager to fulfill the requirements of the law, two individuals show up: Joseph of Arimathea, a Christian in hiding for fear of "the Jews," and Nicodemus, the gentleman of the night. It is hard to miss the ironic (sarcastic?) tone with which the narrator tells of their eagerness to act before night came. Wishing to bury the body of Jesus before sundown, Joseph asks Pilate for the body. Nicodemus comes with one hundred pounds of ointments. Between the two they embalm and bury the body "as is the burial custom of the Jews" (19:40). The following day, we are told, was "a great Sabbath" (19:31). No one has found another reference in the contemporary literature to "a great Sabbath." One hundred pounds of ointment would have been sufficient to embalm a dozen bodies, at a minimum. That they took care to bury the body according to the custom of the Jews tells us that these fellows had not understood the truth of the One who gives the Spirit without measure (3:34). It would appear that the narrator is describing a disoriented concern with "the flesh" by men who live in hiding or in the night and do not have a true connection with the One Sent by the Father. By contrast, in the Synoptics we read that pious women carried out a true act of mercy when they embalmed the dead body of Jesus. The narrative of the anointing and the entombment of Jesus in *According to John* is designed to ridicule two false disciples whose concern with the performance of rituals according to the law is totally misguided. Anxious to get things done properly and before sundown, they show themselves to be unaware of the hour in which they are living.

A short episode in which "the Jews" appear to be sincere in their desire to find out who Jesus really is begins with the annotation, "It was the feast of the Dedication at Jerusalem; it was winter, and Jesus was walking in the temple, in the portico of Solomon" (10:22 – 23). Today the feast of Dedication is known as Hanukkah. It commemorates the re-dedication of the temple after its defilement by the offering of pigs on its altar during the reign of Antiochus Epiphanes. The Maccabean War (167 – 64 BCE), which ended the Syrian rule in Jerusalem and installed the Hasmoneans

Meditations on According to John

in power, culminated with the taking of the temple and its purification from the "abomination that makes desolate" according to Daniel 12:11, or the "desolating sacrilege" of Mark 13:14 and Mt. 24:15. Antiochus had ordered the offering of sacrifices to the Greek god Zeus at the altar of the temple in Jerusalem. This short episode in the gospel, in which Jesus exposes the unbelief of "the Jews" and declares "I and the Father are one" (10:30), causes "the Jews" to take up "stones again to stone him" (10:31). Yes, indeed, at the Feast of Dedication, when "the Jews" celebrate the renewal of the altar at the temple in Jerusalem, it is winter. The fire of the Spirit is not there and the conditions at the temple are very cold. It is difficult to overlook for what purpose the temporal reference is given.

The narrative of the wedding feast at Cana starts with the most significant temporal reference: "On the third day there was a marriage at Cana of Galilee" (2:1). As a chronological marker it is ambiguous. The reader is not informed when to start counting the days. If we become frustrated, however, we are not reading well. For the first Christians, "on the third day" was already a clear reference to the climax of the mission of Jesus.

The Christian confession of faith cited by Paul, known by everyone in his churches, said:

> Christ died for our sins, according to the Scriptures.
> He was buried.
> He was raised on the third day, according to the Scriptures.
> He appeared. (1 Cor. 15:3 – 5)

Here "on the third day" is placed in parallel to "for our sins." The other parallelisms contrast "died" with "was raised" and "was buried" with "appeared." Together "for our sins" and "on the third day" tell us the purpose and the method of the redeeming mission already predicted in the Scriptures.

As an introduction to the narrative of the wedding at Cana, "on the third day" alerts us to the context in which the story is to be understood. Of the actual marriage or the feast that went with it we learn hardly a thing. Apparently the only thing memorable about it was that at the accompanying feast they ran out of wine and Jesus' mother said to him: "They have no wine." It would appear that weddings and wine have always gone together. It was hard to imagine one without the other. Jesus' response to the information provided by his mother gives us a second clue, in case we failed to appreciate the reference to the third day. "Such problem is neither yours nor mine, woman. My hour has not yet come" (2:4, my translation).

By now the reader can surmise that the wine which they do not have will be provided by Jesus when "on the third day" his hour has come. With this already settled, the narrative can proceed. "Now six stone jars were there, for the Jewish rites of purification, each holding twenty or thirty gallons" (2:6). Apparently this was a household in which the purification rituals were rigorously observed and performed very precisely, using running water (not water from a pool or a cistern). We are also told that the six containers were made of stone. These were not fragile pottery jars. Their capacity was also admirable. The Greek says that each jar held two or three *metretas*. Since a *metretés* is the equivalent of 40 liters (almost eleven gallons), each jar had a twenty-seven gallon capacity (100 liters). According to the requirements for purification, of course, the jars were empty.

Jesus ordered the waiters to fill the jars with water, and they filled them up to the brim (the Greek reads "to the above" [2:7] which may be a charged expression). This means that in the jars now there were 600 liters (162 gallons) of water ready to be used for Jewish purification rites. But when the waiters drew from the jars, it was not water. It was wine. The waiters were then told to have the steward approve what was to be served to the guests. The narrator now alerts his readers to an important detail. While the waiters knew where the wine came from, the steward "did not know where it came from." That is, the steward did not know that the wine he had tasted was "water from above." Knowing where Jesus came from is of the essence.

After tasting the wine the steward feels betrayed. He feels that he should have been informed earlier of the existence of such wine. He would have served it first, when the guests would have been able to appreciate it. As it is, he finds himself liable to accusations of incompetence. He not only ignores the details of his job but is also wasting the goods of his master.

According to the steward, it is a misuse of expensive resources to serve the best wine when the guests, who have been drinking an inferior wine, have already lost the ability to enjoy a good wine. The best wine available is served when the guests are in full command of their gustatory talents. Once "drunk" (*methusthósin*, 2:10), any cheap wine may be freely served without fear of losing one's reputation. The steward accuses the bridegroom of not having used his head. His complaint is, "You have kept the good wine until now."

What is this narrative about? Surely it is not primarily about a wedding, of which we do not learn much. It is about a bridegroom who has the best wine available and does not serve it when he should have. Instead, he has waited "until now" to serve the best wine. The narrator tells us that this was the first sign performed by Jesus. Since his hour had not yet come, on the third day, instead of dying on the cross, Jesus manifested his glory providing the best wine at a wedding in which the wine had run out (2:11).

The waiters knew that the wine came from stone jars destined to provide water for the ritual purifications of "the Jews." Of course, those who complain that the bridegroom is a distracted fellow who serves the best wine at the wrong time do not know from whence the best wine comes. The story, in fact, is a well-crafted apologetic parable of the situation faced by the Johannine community. They claim that God did actually wait "until now" to serve the best wine, to bring to humans "grace and truth." "The Jews," of course, claim that God is not a distracted bridegroom who keeps his stewards uninformed. As the efficient steward that he was, Moses served the best wine first, when he gave the law. The Christians insist, to the contrary, that the good wine is to be served "on the third day." When his hour had not yet come, in anticipation of the third day of the cross and resurrection, Jesus at a wedding feast in Cana performed his first sign to awaken the faith of his disciples by providing the one indispensable item that gives life to those celebrating the occasion.

The religion of ritual purifications, the religion of "your law" (10:34; 15:10; 18:31; 19:7), has run out of wine. It has been refurbished with the best wine that is life and truth. Precisely, the irony is that the complaint of the steward, in effect, proclaims the truth of the Gospel. It is necessary to believe in the One Sent by the Father who came "from above" because God waited "until now," "on the third day," to give us life. Christians live "on the third day." This rather elusive time reference that sets the stage for understanding the changing of water into wine, does not just set the time for a wedding feast. Christians celebrate life, what all weddings promise, drinking the wine of the gospel. Rather than being a religion that regulates life with purification rituals, the religion of Christ is the celebration of the triumph of life "on the third day."

10
I Finished the Work

In the synoptic gospels Jesus' healings and exorcisms are called *dynamis*. English versions translate this term as "wonder," "virtue," "miracle." The Greek word means "strength," "power." The words "dynamo" and "dynamite" are derived from it.

In *According to Mark* we also read that the Pharisees, wishing to test Jesus, asked him for a "sign from heaven." Finding himself under attack, Jesus, being quite disturbed, said: "Why does this generation seek a sign? Truly, I say to you, no sign shall be given to this generation" (Mk. 8:11). Apparently his visit to Dalmanutha consisted of this brief and terse encounter. On the other side of the Sea of Galilee Jesus had fed four thousand with seven loaves of bread and a few fishes. We do not know whether the people of Dalmanutha knew about that miracle. Of course, the fact that the Pharisees were "testing" or "tempting" Jesus by asking for a sign from heaven may explain Jesus' sharp negation. That they sought a sign, a *semeia,* and not a *dynamis,* does tell us something. It would seem that a distinction is being made between a demonstration of power and a sign.

This saying of Jesus is also recorded, under different circumstances, in *According to Matthew* 12:39 – 40 and in *According to Luke* 11:29. In these versions of the saying Jesus makes an exception: "but no sign shall be given to it except the sign of the prophet Jonah" (Mt. 12:39). In *According to Luke* the context gives the impression that the sign of Jonah is that of the preacher who announces judgment to Gentiles. *According to Matthew* points out that Jonah survived three days in the sea protected by a great fish used by God for this purpose. Symbolically, of course, the sea is the source and the power of evil and death. In the apocalyptic literature the powers that rise against God come from the sea. Here it says that, like Jonah in the belly of the great fish in the midst of the sea, the Son of man is to spend three days protected by God "in the heart of the earth." The sign of Jonah, evidently, has to do with his survival in the realm of death.

In the gospel *According to John* the miracles of Jesus are not called *dynamis*, but *semeia*. They are signs. We already noticed in a previous meditation that the transformation of water into wine is identified as the first sign. In the second half of this chapter (2:13 – 22), Jesus makes a great demonstration of power by expelling from the temple the merchants and money changers. The reaction of "the Jews" is to ask, "What sign have you to show us for doing this?" Jesus' answer is: "Destroy this temple, and in three days I will raise it up." This is another Johannine saying with double meaning that is misunderstood. The narrator explains, "But he spoke of the temple of his body" and then states that the disciples remembered this saying when he was raised from the dead. This would seem to be a different version of what in *According to Matthew* is presented as the sign of Jonah. In this case, the details show that by asking for a sign "the Jews" were revealing their blindness before the sign they had witnessed. But in both cases the request for a sign is answered by a reference to his passage through the realm of death.

In *According to Mark* the miracles (*dynamis*) are demonstrations of power that cause the witnesses to recognize that their doer has a special connection with God. In the Old Testament there are prophets who distinguished themselves more for their miracles than for their oracles. The best example is Elisha. Jesus is recognized as a prophet because he performs miracles in the tradition of Elijah and Elisha. The Jewish literature of Jesus' time tells of contemporaneous miracle workers who also actualized this tradition.

In *According to John*, however, the whole narrative is an argument that Jesus is not a prophet, a human being with a double portion of the Spirit and a special connection with God. He does not perform miracles. He gives signs. The difference is important. The miracle has significance in itself. The sign points toward something other than itself. In *According to Mark* the expulsion of the merchants from the temple causes the chief priests to decide to kill Jesus. The story is framed by the cursing of the fig tree, the symbol of Israel (Mk. 11:12 – 22). In *According to John* the expulsion of the merchants has nothing to do with the decision to kill him. It signals a change of the cosmic center (the temple) from a building in Jerusalem to the body of the Risen One. It is a sign that points to the new life of the one who will spend three days "in the heart of the earth." It is the sign of Jonah.

As the transformation of water into wine means the transition from the religion of rites to the religion of life, the expulsion of the merchants means the passage from a material cosmos to a spiritual one. A new temple is a new cosmos. The relationship of human beings with God from now on takes place in a structure different from the temple of Jerusalem. Both signs point to the radical transformation of the universe in which human beings live thanks to the glorification of the Son of man.

In *According to John* the signs are not intended to cause the witnesses to believe that Jesus is a prophet with supernatural powers that allow him to communicate the word of God or to do things that break the limits of nature. He is not a wonder worker. He gives signs, and their function is to bring about the recognition of the crucified as the glorified, the only one who has ascended to heaven because he is also the only one who descended from heaven. Informing his Father that he has fulfilled his mission, Jesus declares that his disciples "know in truth that I came from thee, and they have believed that thou didst send me" (17:8).

The signs point to THE SIGN. The crucifixion and the resurrection, the events on the third day, comprise the object needed by faith. They are the way by which the Son returns to the Father and the way in which those of faith live in the presence of God. Consequently the narrator, conscious that the cross and the life of the Risen One change the cosmic reality, explains: "When therefore he was raised from the dead, the disciples remembered that he had said this, and they believed" (2:22). Was it impossible to believe in Him before the resurrection? — that is, to believe that he was the one sent by the Father, the one who descended from heaven?

We are told that the signs were meant to produce faith, even if indirectly. The transformation of water into wine, identified as the first sign, caused the disciples to believe (2:11). The expulsion of the merchants from the temple, when later remembered, caused the disciples to believe (2:22). The healing of the son of the Roman official from Capernaum, identified as the second sign, caused the official and his household to believe (4:53). At the end of the gospel the narrator affirms that he provided enough signs to cause the readers to believe (20:30). For the members of the Johannine community, surely, the signs were arrows that pointed to "the third day." Those who see the "sign of Jonah" are true disciples.

Obviously, however, before his glorification on the cross (I can't think of a greater oxymoron), the signs were ambiguous. They did not automatically produce faith. The narrative of this gospel is characterized, among other things, by not introducing the reader to the story little by little, opening up the plot and its meaning in a way that the reader can reasonably follow to the desired conclusion. The way the material is here presented, from the very beginning the reader must have full knowledge of the symbolic universe of the plot if understanding of the story is to be gained at all. Only those who believe that the crucified has been glorified by the Father can see the signs for what they are.

The consequence of the expulsion of the merchants from the temple was that "many believed in his name when they saw the signs which he did" (2:23). The narrator warns us, however, that Jesus did not trust their faith (2:24 – 25), and Nicodemus, who comes to Jesus attracted by the signs but in the night so as not to be seen by "the Jews," is their representative. He recognizes that only one who has a special connection with God can perform them (3:2). However, when Jesus instructs him not to give importance to earthly things (miracles), Nicodemus becomes disoriented and asks, "How can this be?" (3:9). Then he disappears into the night from whence he came. "Jesus knew from the first who those were that did not believe" (6:64).

Later in the story we read that a multitude was following Jesus because they had seen signs and healings and therefore declared him to be "a prophet" (6:2 -4). This reaction, undoubtedly, is not sufficient. After the raising of Lazarus, the chief priests and the Pharisees gathered the council because they were concerned by the fact that "this man performs many signs" (11:47). Their decision, of course, was not to believe. Rather, they decided to kill him.

Those who joyously receive him in Jerusalem, while the authorities are seeking to kill him, have been influenced by the sign of the raising of Lazarus (12:18). They had heard of Lazarus' resurrection and wished to see him as he was coming to Jerusalem with Jesus (12:9). The chief priests now planned also to put Lazarus to death (12:10). The curiosity of the multitude, however, was not faith.

As in chapter six so also in chapter twelve we read that the signs do not produce faith. Chapter six begins with the report that "a multitude followed him because they saw the signs which he did on those who were diseased" (6:2). Jesus reproves those who ate of the bread and the fish on the other side of the Sea of Galilee and followed him to Capernaum, declaring, "You seek me not because you saw signs, but because you ate your fill of the loaves" (6:26). Their reaction to the miraculous feeding was to wish to make him king (6:14 – 15), a misguided endeavor. Of those who know of Lazarus' resurrection and receive Jesus triumphantly into Jerusalem, the narrator comments that even though Jesus had done "so many signs before them, yet they did not believe in him" (12:37).

To give the picture another twist, *According to John* says that Jesus told those who did not believe in him that at least they should believe in his "works" (*erga*), again avoiding the word miracle, or wonder (*dynamis*). His works give testimony of who he is. In his heated polemic with "the Jews," Jesus affirms, "The works that I do in my Father's name, they bear witness to me" (10:25). "I have shown you many good works from the Father; for which of these do you stone me" (10:32)? "If I am not doing the works of my Father, then do not believe me; but if I do them, ... believe the works" (10:37 – 38). It would seem, then, that the works, like the signs, produce the opposite of what is intended.

In a farewell discourse, Jesus explains to his disciples that the reason why "the Jews" hate both him and his Father is because they have seen his works. If they had not seen his works, they would be without sin, but because they have seen the works he does in his Father's name, they are condemned (15:24). This judgment, however, leaves us somewhat perplexed because in this gospel it is made clear that only those whom the Father has delivered into his hand can come to him. "No one can come to me unless the Father who sent me draws him" (6:44). And those who have been delivered to him by his Father cannot be snatched out of his hand (10:28 – 29). The narrator also tells us that those who saw the signs did not believe so that the Scripture might be fulfilled (15:25). If this is the case, how can those who do not believe be held responsible?

When "the Jews" accuse him of breaking the Sabbath by ordering the paralytic at the Pool of Bethesda to carry his bed home after having been healed, Jesus informs them that the Father shows the Son everything he does, "and greater works than these will he show him, that you may marvel" (5:20). The greater works he performs are those of giving life and of judging, two exclusive divine prerogatives, as pointed out in the following verses (5:21 – 30). By being in the world performing signs Jesus is like a coin that can indicate "heads or tails." Confronted by the one performing signs, people get either life or condemnation. The signs produce either faith or unbelief.

In his farewell prayer Jesus affirms, "I glorified thee on earth, having accomplished the work which thou gavest me to do" (17:4). Long before, by the well of Jacob, he had announced to his disciples, "My food is to do the will of him who sent me, and to accomplish his work" (4:34)). That he did accomplish the will of the Father who sent him is confirmed by the last word pronounced by Jesus on the cross, "It is finished" (19:30). That is, it has been accomplished. His signs do not make prominent the virtues, the powers of a miracle worker. They signal the consummation of his work, which he described as the food that sustained his life. Jesus' work was consummated when he was lifted up, on the third day, on the cross.

It is, therefore, somewhat disconcerting to read the promise Jesus makes to those who believe in him: "He who believes in me will also do the works that I do; and even greater works than these will he do, because I go to the Father" (14:12). The work of Jesus was to enact the sign of Jonah by living to do the will of God, something that Jonah had much difficulty in understanding and accepting. By contrast, Jesus understood and fully accepted the purpose of his life. He accomplished the work he was assigned. At the end he was able to truthfully say, "It is finished." What greater work can be done by the one who believes in him? I don't think the members of the Johannine community supposed that they would be performing miracles (*dynamis*) greater than those Jesus had performed. Rather, they saw themselves as witnesses to The Truth and understood that their hour would also come. At that time they would have to work out the sign that points to the work of the one glorified on the cross. Their food, that which sustained their lives, was their determination to transpose the words that Jesus had spoken to them into life-giving works. For them, his words were "spirit and life" (6:63) when incarnated into their lives. They were to give signs that called attention to the one who was in "the heart of the earth" for three days. In the lives of the faithful the connection of their works to their ultimate purpose in life must not be ambiguous.

Jesus lived performing signs that pointed to the time when he would finish his work. Therefore the life of the Christian must provide signs that advertise the source of strength and vision for those who live by faith. Signs and faith must remain closely bound in the lives of the disciples of the one who is THE SIGN that must be seen and believed.

11

THE LAW WAS GIVEN THROUGH MOSES

The reader who wishes to fully understand *According to John* must have a good knowledge of the Old Testament. The way in which the stories and the discourses of Jesus are structured reflects patterns and themes prominent in the Jewish Scriptures. As noticed in a previous meditation, the narrator assumes that the reader knows the significance of Old Testament festivals and will thereby realize the meaning of pivotal words and acts of Jesus. It is, therefore, somewhat surprising to note how this gospel radically re-defines the will of God.

In the Prologue a marked contrast is made between Moses and the law on the one hand, and Jesus Christ and grace and truth on the other (1:17). In fact, this verse contrasts three things, and the three remain in apposition throughout the gospel: Jesus Christ is contrasted with Moses, the law is contrasted with grace and truth, and "was given" is contrasted with "was actualized" or "came to be." Aligning these contrasts we learn that grace and truth are present in the person of Jesus Christ. By contrast, Moses is the agent of the law. This distinction is fundamental.

The contrasts are re-affirmed by the way in which the law is always attached to Moses. It is his law and, as such, "their law" (8:17; 10:34; 18:31), the law of "the Jews." Actually, the law is not the expression of God's mind or will. Mercy and truth, the essential divine qualities, are not found in it. That "the Jews" expect to find truth and life in it is their basic misconception. In *According to John,* Jesus describes their attitude and expectations only to turn the tables on them. One of his many charges against "the Jews" is that they are searching for life in the Scriptures. They are looking for the right thing in the wrong place. Life can be found only in him. He is where mercy, truth and life are actualized (5:39).

"The Jews" consider Moses, their law giver, to be their savior. They have placed their hope in him (5:45). Their hope, however, is misplaced. Hope can stand only on faith. For their hope to be genuine they would have to believe in Moses. But, Jesus accuses them of failing to believe in Moses (5:46). If they believed in Moses they would have found out that the law does not give life. It gives, rather, testimony to Jesus (5:39). The result of their failure to believe in Moses is that their hope in Moses will be their undoing. Instead of being their advocate, their defense attorney (*Parákletos*), Moses will turn out to be their District Attorney, their accuser (5:45).

This characterization of Moses and his law, no doubt, is one developed by Christians who have come to see the Living Christ as "the Savior of the world" (4:42), not just the lawgiver of the Jews. Honesty would demand admitting that the Scriptures claim to be the fountain of life for the people of God. Psalm 119, for instance, is a long paean to the virtues of the law, and all the Deuteronomic literature is an argument for God's retributive justice as operative on the standard of the law. For the Deuteronomists God's blessings are dependent on obedience to the commandments. The point of view of the Johannine community, it must be admitted, is clearly polemical. "The Jews" are not only misguided in thinking that they will find life in the law. Even if that were possible, they would not receive life from the law on account of their failure to keep it. There is a clear sarcastic tone in the voice that asks, "Did not Moses give you the law? Yet none of you keeps the law" (7:19).

The new understanding of the Father's action in the death and the life of the Son gave Christians a new understanding of the role of the law. On the one hand, they recognized that the presence of the Spirit among them superseded the possession of a law which, in the words of Paul, Jews had taken to be "the embodiment of knowledge and truth" (Rom. 2:20). Christians now saw that salvation, life, could only be found in the incarnate *Logos*. Still, they could not throw the law out the window or consign all copies of it to a store room for eventual dissolution. They could only understand the significance of Jesus' life and death with the Scriptures as their guide. Indeed, the context provided by "Moses in the law and [by] the prophets" (1:45) was essential. Thus, both for Paul and for the Johannine community the law's function is redefined as a witness to the mission of Jesus. *According to John* is quite radical in this regard. To the Jews, as Paul says, sin is defined by the law. If that is the case there is no sin where there is no law. Paul finds a new way to define sin: "whatever does not proceed from faith is sin" (Rom. 14:23). In this gospel sin is defined by a discreet reference to the One Sent by the Father. The presence of the Son in the world exposes as sinners all those who reject him.

The irony of the situation is that those who think that life is given by the law use it to condemn Jesus as a sinner worthy of death. On the basis of their application of the law to daily life, Jesus is a sinner who mixed water and dirt making mud on a Sabbath. They base their refusal to believe in him on his being a sinner. They know for sure that God does not listen to sinners (9:31). On the contrary, they are absolutely certain that God had spoken to Moses (9:29). Their dependence on Moses, however, prevents them from believing, either in Moses or in the One Sent. Based on their unfounded certainty it is clear to them that Jesus' claim to being the Word Sent by the Father is not to be believed. Security based on traditional authority may turn out to be not only false but also a barrier to the avenues for the consideration of new evidence.

More specifically, Jesus not only claims to be the Word Sent by the Father, he makes himself equal with God. In the eyes of "the Jews," therefore, he is a blasphemer (10:36). On this account, they report to Pilate that "according to our law he is to die" (19:7).

This is highly ironic. The law in which "the Jews" seek to find life, is the one they use to pronounce Jesus a sinner and condemn him to death. They have turned things upside down. On the one hand, Moses, from whom they hope to receive life and to whom they appeal to condemn Jesus to death, is their accuser instead. On the other hand, the one they accuse by appeals to Moses is the actual giver of life.

Paul agrees to the condemnatory power of the law. He says, "the law brings wrath, but where there is no law there is no transgression" (Rom. 4:15). As an apocalypticist he is concerned primarily about God's justice and God's wrath (Rom. 1:17 – 18). The power of the law over sinners activates God's wrath. *According to John* is not primarily concerned with the justice or the wrath of God. Therefore, this gospel does not present the cross as the means by which the power of the law, which is energized by sin and death (1Cor. 15:56), is broken. A Christianity that is primarily concerned with retributive justice has seen the cross primarily in legal terms. From this perspective, at the cross God demonstrated that justice works. It is the ransom paid for the release of those imprisoned by the law in the realm of sin and death (Mk. 10:45). In the words of an early hymn quoted by Paul, Christ's "obedience unto death, even death on a cross" (Phil. 2:8) is what gives power to the gospel (Rom. 1:16).

The symbolic universe of *According to John* is not apocalyptic, and justice is not its ultimate concern. Here we are in the universe of the Father's grace and truth actualized in the life and death of the Son. The law has nothing to do with the bestowal of eternal life. Human beings are not required to crucify themselves with Christ in order to be redeemed from the power of the law, as understood by Paul (Gal. 2:20; Rom. 8:1). Rather, the cross is the way by which the Son ascended in his return to the Father. Eternal life is now available to humanity on account of the incarnation, the actualization of grace and truth in the world below, which culminated with the "glorification" on the cross. Eternal life is bestowed on those who hear the voice of the Shepherd who leads his sheep out to good pastures and eternal union with the life of God (10:4).

In this way, the gospel bypasses the law and its function in a universal system of justice. The role of Moses as the lawgiver is to be recognized to a degree, but it cannot be granted pride of place as was the case in Judaism. In *According to John* "the Jews" claim that Moses gave them bread from heaven, but Jesus denies the effectiveness of Moses' bread (6:32). The real bread from heaven and the real living water were not given by Moses at all. The bread and the water given by Moses were temporary and perishable. Their effectiveness was limited to the world below. By contrast, life in the Spirit, provided and maintained by the true bread from heaven, is now available to those who believe in the Son.

In this gospel Jesus proclaims a "new" commandment (13:34), which is also referred to as "my" commandment: "that you love one another" (15:12). Again, Paul agrees: "Love one another; for he who loves his neighbor has fulfilled the law" (Rom. 13:8). Furthermore, Jesus identifies his mission as the fulfillment of a commandment received from the Father (20:18). His commandment, therefore, is to be traced directly to God, unlike the law of "the Jews" which is credited to Moses. As a consequence, and in direct contrast, the commandment which the Son received from the Father is eternal life (12:50). There is life in "my commandment."

According to John promises that all those who keep "my word" will never see death (8:51). Keeping "my word" is defined as loving Jesus. It is not a matter of obedience, but of love. The positive expression of the promise says: "If a man loves me, he will keep my word, and my Father will love him, and we will come to him and make our home with him" (14:23). The consequence of keeping "my word" is not just the avoidance of death. It is the privilege of living at home with the Father and the Son who reinforce their love with those who respond with love to the Father's loving initiative (3:16).

What Jesus calls "my word" is in reality, as he tells the Father in prayer, "thy word" (17:14), which is "the Truth." In his farewell prayer Jesus asks the Father to "sanctify them in the truth; thy word is truth" (17:17). We already know, because the prologue told us, that grace and truth are actualized in Jesus Christ, the *Logos*, the Word (1:17). The truth that sanctifies is not in the law, but in the incarnate Word. The law had been the instrument of sanctification for post-exilic Judaism. It is what distinguished the people of God from other nations, dividing humanity into Jews and Gentiles. The frontier that divided humanity into Jews and Gentiles was the law. By the end of the first century, mainstream Christianity had come to agree that the law was no longer the instrument with which to define the people of God. Jews and Gentiles are no longer separated by a wall or any other barrier, as was the case in the Jerusalem temple (Eph. 2:14 – 15). Gentiles are full members of the people of God. In *According to John* the law that identifies a people separate from "the Gentiles" has been replaced by an incarnate Word that sanctifies a people who is not "of the world" but is to be witnesses "in the world" (17:14 – 17).

Those sanctified by the Word are not a special group set apart from the rest of the community who are thereby authorized to function as priest in a temple. Rather, the sanctification of the whole community, where love has broken all barriers separating Jews from Gentiles or priests and Levites from the rest of the people, has given to the community a totally new identity and standing before God. In this gospel the trigger that sets in motion the road to Calvary is the need for "the Greeks" to see Jesus (12:20 – 21). In this way the privileged position of the Jews who had the law of Moses as their most precious possession, and as the source of claims for exclusive access to God's grace, has been obviously set aside. *According to John* makes clear that the Johannine community had admitted Gentiles to full membership. The love that demonstrates the ties that bind the Christian community defines and unites people in a much more effective way than that which a law could ever accomplish. The will of God had been fully accomplished by the Son when he was lifted up, and thereby those who believe in the Son as the One Sent by the Father receive life. In this symbolic universe the law of

Moses does no longer have a saving role. It only serves to illumine the saving role of the Son sent by the Father.

12

I Have Overcome the World

In the gospel *According to John* the word "world" is, without a doubt, semantically rich. This word appears more than sixty times in the text, and if one does not pay attention it is relatively easy to misinterpret the message of the gospel or conclude that it contradicts itself. It is necessary, therefore, to explore its semantic range.

To begin with, we may note that in several places "world" is used to refer to a multitude, the masses, the people. Because of the wide publicity given to the raising of Lazarus, the Pharisees worry that "the world has gone after him" (12:19). When Jesus' brothers advise him to go up to Jerusalem for the feast of Tabernacles, they say; "show yourself to the world" (7:4). Being interrogated by Pilate about his disciples and his doctrines, Jesus answers: "I have spoken openly to the world; I have always taught in synagogues and in the temple where all Jews come together; I have said nothing secretly" (18:20). In these instances the world is the public space where people come together. It is the opposite of a secret place. This usage of the word is an argument against those who picture Jesus as the dispenser of esoteric, secret knowledge.

World is also used in the more literal sense of the Greek word *kosmos*, referring to creation. In the beginning verses we read that the world "was made through him" (1:10). The one who made it also became flesh so, it is said, he "is coming into the world" (11:27). "Before the world was made," however, the Son already had glory in the presence of the Father (17:5, 24). With characteristic double meaning, Jesus reminds his disciples that the day has twelve hours, and it is necessary to walk during the day, seeing "the light of this world" in order not to stumble. It is clear that he is referring to the sun, but then he is no longer referring to it when he adds: "If any one walks in the night, he stumbles, because the light is not in him" (11:9 – 10).

The world is also a reference to humanity, that aspect of creation with which God has a special relationship. In this relationship the love of God plays a decisive role. As is well said by the best known text in this gospel, "God so loved the world that he gave his only Son, that whoever believes in him should … have eternal life" (3:16). In order to make points in an implicit debate, the narrator adds: "For God sent the Son into the world, not to condemn the world, but that the world might be saved through him" (3:17). While verse sixteen affirms that only those who believe in him receive eternal life, verse seventeen affirms that he came to save the world, that is, humanity. As Jesus says to Pilate: "For this I was born, and for this I have come into the world" (18:37). The tension between these two affirmations is left unresolved.

In his farewell prayer Jesus envisions those who will believe through the word of his disciples after his return to the Father. It is necessary that the believers of future generations be united in the same way in which the Father and the Son are united. The unity of the disciples is to cause the world to believe that he is the One Sent by the Father (17:20 – 21). The unity of the Father with the Son, of the Son with his disciples and of his disciples with those who believe through their word will cause the world to "know that thou hast sent me and hast loved them even as thou hast loved me" (17:23). The love of God for humanity (the world) that is manifest in the unity of the Father, the Son and those who believe will cause humanity to know that he is the One Sent by the Father.

The love of God for humanity is particularly anchored in those who believe. This is expressed well by means of the image of the Son as the bread that descended from heaven. While those who ate of the manna provided by Moses received earthly life, those who eat of this bread "will live for ever; and the bread which I shall give for the life of the world is my flesh" (6:51, cp. 6:33). Granting that Jesus will give his flesh (his life in the world below) "for the life of the world," only those who eat of this bread will live forever. Thus, the ambiguity noticed above remains in place.

It must be admitted, however, that many human beings refuse to eat the bread from heaven. They are unbelievers, and this cohort is also referred to as the world. Already in the first verses we read that "the world knew him not" (1:10). When Jesus promises to send the Paraclete, the Spirit of Truth, to his disciples, he concedes that "the world cannot receive [him], because it neither sees him nor knows him" (14:16 -17). Later he warns them, "If the world hates you, know that it has hated me before it hated you" (15:18). In his farewell prayer Jesus laments, "O righteous Father, the world has not known thee" (17:25). It is clear, then, that the world in which God is not known and which rejects both the Son and the Paraclete is not the world of those who believe and receive eternal life.

Even though the Father did not send the Son to condemn the world of humanity (3:17; 12:47), the world of those who do not know the Father, and hate the Son and those who believe in him, has been judged and condemned. The presence of the Son in the world of humanity makes him the agent of judgment (5:22). "Truly, truly, I say to you, he who hears my word and believes him who sent me, has eternal life; he does not come into judgment, but has passed from death to life" (5:24). On the other hand, he who refuses to believe (*ho apeithon*) in the Son "shall not see life, but the wrath of God rests upon him" (3:36). The lifting up of the Son on the cross is the crisis of the world. At this event humanity is divided into two worlds. As Jesus tells the Pharisees who accuse him of breaking the Sabbath by making mud to heal the man born blind: "For judgment I came into this world" (9:39). Later, when the Greeks request to see Jesus, he announces: "Now is the judgment of this world" (12:31). The world of humanity is divided into the world of faith and the world of unbelief by the presence of the Son.

Sometimes the word world is used to refer to the human condition in the sphere below, where biological death is a fact of life. Jesus, however, demoted this death to just "sleep" (11:11). In his polemic with "the Jews" Jesus says to them: "You are from below, I am from above; you are of this world, I am not of this world" (8:23). The life of the incarnate *Logos* is his passage through the world below. "I came from the Father and have come into the world; again, I am leaving the world and going to the Father" (16:28). While he is leaving the world below and returning to the world above, his disciples remain in the world below. On their behalf, Jesus asks the Father: "I do not pray that thou shouldst take them out of the world, but that thou shouldst keep them from the evil one" (17:15).

Here a distinction is being made between the world below, in which Jesus lived and his disciples will continue to live even while in possession of eternal life, and the "fallen" world that is under the power of the Evil One. In the case of Judas, the Evil One is identified as the Devil (13:2) or Satan (13:27), but on three occasions he is named "the ruler of this world." As Jesus points out, however, this ruler "has no power over me" (14:30), and has been "cast out" or "judged" (12:31; 16:11). This is the ruler of evil and eschatological death. While still living in the world below where the Evil One may disturb their lives, Jesus' disciples do not live in a world under the power of the Evil One. On this account Jesus concludes his second Farewell Discourse declaring, "In the world you have tribulation; but be of good cheer, I have overcome the world" (16:33). The world over which he triumphed is the world of eschatological death.

The world that has been overcome is the world of the ruler of evil, and those of faith do not live in that world. They have eternal life, even while living in the world below, where tribulations may persist. Jesus makes the point by telling his disciples "you are not of this world, but I chose you out of the world" (15:19), that is, out of the fallen world. The fallen world is not the same as the world below. This differentiation also accounts for the observation "he who hates his life in this world will keep it for eternal life" (12:25). The one who hates his life in the world ruled by the Evil One can continue to live in the world below enjoying eternal life.

Taking this distinction into account, Jesus can also compare the way in which the Father sent him to the way in which he is sending his disciples: "As thou didst send me into the world, so I have sent them into the world" (17:18, cp. 20:21). Of course, while the Father sent him from the world above to the world below, he is sending his disciples from the world below to the world of unbelief.

The fallen world is the world conceived by apocalypticism in order to maintain the doctrine of God's retributive justice. In its literature we find descriptions of mythological battles that culminate in the great battle of Armageddon. Only after this triumph can God deal with each one according to their deeds. Apocalypticism affirms that the justice of God will finally reveal itself in the life of the saints after the resurrection, not in the life of the saints who live in the present evil world.

According to John represents the Wisdom tradition best expressed in *Job*. Both *Job* and *According to John* have a cosmic view of reality. They view God in reference to creation, but they reject the apocalyptic vision, which is also universalistic. Theirs is not the apocalyptic God. Their God is the God of unity, confraternity, peace and life. Not the God of vengeance, and of armies that triumph in the battlefields. In this gospel we do not read about the separation of the sheep and the goats, a great Assize in heaven, the signs that announce a future *Parousia*, wars and rumors of wars and the desolating abomination. The parables of the kingdom that center on a prominent apocalyptic metaphor and are essential to the message of Jesus in the synoptic gospels are here absent.

While tacitly admitting that "the ruler of this world" has enjoyed freedom of action until now, the glorification of the Son has cast him out. Eternal life is lived now by the believers, and the wrath of God already rests on the unbelievers. While admitting that life in the world below has afflictions, it affirms that those who believe have peace (16:33) because the Son has been victorious over the fallen world where eschatological death reigns ("I have overcome" in Greek is in the perfect tense, as "It is finished" in 19:30).

This Johannine perspective in its essence informs the way in which the tradition of Jesus' walking on the sea is told:

> Since it was getting late, the disciples went down to the sea, embarked in a small boat, and were coming from the opposite shore to Capernaum. It had already become dark and Jesus had not come to them, but the sea was agitated by strong winds. Having already gone between twenty-five and thirty stadia, they saw Jesus walking on the sea close to the boat, and they became afraid. Jesus, however, said to them: 'I am, do not be afraid.' They then wished to receive him in the boat, but immediately the boat arrived at the land to which it was going (6:16 – 21, my translation).

The theme of this account is not Jesus' calming of the storm. Here the disciples are in the middle of the sea of Galilee, between twenty five and thirty stadia from the eastern shore. It is night, and a strong wind is fueling a storm in the sea, but the disciples are not afraid of the storm. They become afraid when they see someone walking on the sea as its master.

When Jesus identifies himself saying "I am," two things happen. 1) Their fear is gone, and they wish that Jesus would join them in the boat. 2) Their wish is frustrated because miraculously the boat has arrived at their destination. This makes it unnecessary for Jesus to enter the boat or calm the storm. This story tells us that those who receive an epiphany of the one who triumphed over the prince of this world no longer find themselves in the sea of the world ruled by the ruler of this world. They have arrived at the harbor they wished to reach, even if they do not have Jesus in the boat with them. They are still in the world below. This version of the story reveals the theological perspective of *According to John*.

The disciples in the boat—which is the agent of salvation — are in the darkness and in a stormy sea, the realm of death. As Jesus said to them, "In the world you have tribulation; but be of good cheer, I have overcome the world." The One who walks over the sea, the source and the power of evil and death, takes his disciples out of the sea. They miraculously find themselves at the harbor to which they were going. They have the life and the peace that the Son came to give them. He says to them: "Do not be afraid.... Peace I leave with you; my peace I give to you. Not as the world gives I give to you. Let not your hearts be troubled, neither let them be afraid.... I have said this to you, that in me you may have peace" (6:20; 14:27; 16:33). They continue to be in the world below, but like Jesus, they are not part of the fallen world. Their faith has transplanted them to the land where they wished to go. They live in the peaceful world of the Risen One.

The eschatology of *According to John* is not apocalyptic. Instead of being at the service of the desire to understand God's justice and how the future will reveal it, its eschatology is controlled by its Christology. The presence of the incarnate *Logos* in the world makes salvation a reality now. As such it is effective in the community that while living in the world is not of the world. The Son who came to all these worlds did not leave having accomplished only the first stage of his mission, so as to leave its cosmic aspects for some future time. With full assurance and sincerity he said: "I have finished the work which thou gavest me to do" (17:4). Those who believe in him live the more abundant life (10:10) in the world below in peace. In this gospel Jesus does not predict a great miraculous demonstration of power (*dynamis*) to be performed by him at his future return in glory and majesty. Rather, Jesus predicts "greater works" to be realized by his disciples in the world below after he has accomplished his work in that world (14:12).

The believers commissioned to do these greater works continue to live in the world below, but not in the fallen world of eschatological death. They actually live in the world (*kosmos*) represented by the temple of the body of the Risen Christ (2:21). As I said in a previous meditation, a new temple is a new cosmos. It is in the new world of the Risen Body, where the life and the peace of Christ reign, that the believers live even as they are also in the world of humanity and the world of the human condition where biological death is a fact of life. As witnesses to the Truth they live in several worlds. The gospel's central doctrine, the incarnation, is an affirmation of the value of humanity and the world below. Since the Son descended and became incarnate in order to ascend, the gospel also affirms that Jesus came to the world to create the new world of the Spirit where worship takes place in the temple of the body of The Glorified.

13
It Is Not by Measure that God Gives the Spirit

The four cherubim seen by Ezekiel riding on wheels and crossing the heavens shining with God's glory (Ez. 1:10; 10:14) were also seen by John the Theologian next to the throne of God (Rev. 4:6-7). Their faces were that of a lion, an ox, a man and an eagle. Not long afterwards Christians adopted these four creatures to represent the four gospels. *According to John* was given the eagle as its icon. The exact reason for this choice is not known, but later it was justified by noting the eagle's capacity to soar high in the heavens, higher than any other bird.

As early as the beginning of the third century, Clement of Alexandria singled out *According to John* as the gospel that presents the spiritual realities of the ministry of Jesus. As an eagle, this gospel soars to the heights where, according to the cosmology of the chain of being, are found the spiritual realities which rise above the material world. Because of this explicit preference for the realm of the Spirit, there has never been a shortage of those who think that this gospel represents an idealistic escape from material reality.

The prologue of this gospel focuses on the spiritual, eternal realities of the world of light and life (1:4). There the *Logos* was with God, and was God. After stating that the *Logos* was made flesh and dwelt among humans to bring to them grace and truth (1:14), the narrative begins with the testimony of John. His function is not to baptize Jesus but to proclaim that he saw the Spirit descend as a dove on him (1:32-33). Here Jesus and John the Baptist do not have a personal encounter. John saw Jesus from some distance and identified him as the Lamb of God who takes away the sin of the world (1:29). We do not read that Jesus received a water baptism. John's role is to identify Jesus as the one who is to baptize with the Spirit (1:33). In this way John publicly testifies of the arrival of both the *Logos* and the Spirit to the world below. Jesus is not portrayed as one whose life is fully integrated into the world where sinning takes place and baptism for the remission of sins is necessary.

In the first farewell discourse Jesus promises to send his disciples "another" Comforter (*Parákletos,* 14:16). Thus, it is reasonable to think that the One who descended from heaven and on whom the Spirit came down as a dove is the first Comforter, precisely because he made possible the descent of the Spirit. The "other" Comforter will be able only to descend to the world below when the *Logos* had ascended and returned to the world above from whence he came. It is lamentable that the Greek word *Parákletos* has been translated as "comforter." Even though this English word fits within the semantic range of the Greek word, it reduces the connotations of the original so as to give a false impression. The Greek word also says Consoler, Advocate, Defense Attorney, One Ready to Help, Protector. These other senses also apply to the uses of *Parákletos* in the farewell discourses.

The presence of the Spirit in the world below in the person of the One Who Descended makes not only possible but even necessary that women and men be born, not just baptized, from water and from the Spirit. That is, they must be born "from above" (3:3). The Greek word *anothen* means both "from above" and "once again." Which of its senses is the one intended is determined by the context. In his conversation with Nicodemus, Jesus avails himself of the double sense of the word to bring out Nicodemus' inability to understand that Jesus is not talking about earthly births (3:12).

A birth from human parents produces life "in the flesh." A birth from water and the Spirit produces life "in the Spirit." The activity of the Spirit is illumined by a metaphor. It is like the activity of the wind that blows without anyone's knowing where it comes from and where it is going. In other words, it is mysterious, a miracle. As many other things in the realm of nature, however, with the advances made by science in recent centuries the activity of the wind has ceased being mysterious. Television station meteorologists explain to their viewers the atmospheric conditions and the causes for the way in which the wind is blowing and predict the direction and the strength with which it will blow tomorrow. The metaphor used to illustrate the way in which the Spirit works in *According to John* no longer has the same effect. The coming and going of the wind is now understood as the result of differences in atmospheric pressures and the earth's rotation. There is no mystery there. But the way in which the birth "from above" is brought about by the activity of the Spirit continues to be a mystery and produces a miracle. Even though in the realm of the flesh the activity of the wind can be predicted, the work of the Spirit of God continues to be unpredictable and miraculous.

The distinction between the flesh and the Spirit is at the very center of the Johannine universe. "That which is born of the flesh is flesh, and that which is born of the Spirit is spirit" (3:6). This may not make sense when understood in natural terms, but is easily understood by those who see the world as God's creation. When reality is seen not in terms of nature, but of creation, the birth that only the Spirit can produce is still mysterious, but reasonable. To make possible the crossing of the abyss between life in the flesh and life in the Spirit is the purpose for which the Son came to live among women and men and thus unite them to their Creator.

This contrast is also defined in practical terms: "It is the Spirit that gives life, the flesh is of no avail; the words I have spoken to you are spirit and life" (6:63). The Spirit and life, no doubt, are inseparable. Being born to life in the flesh is transitory and perilous. By contrast, being born to life in the Spirit is certainly effective and produces life eternal in human beings who still live in the flesh. Its characterization as "more abundant" (10:10) does not refer to its quantity but to its quality. That is, human beings who have been born of the Spirit can also soar to spiritual heights like a dove or an eagle and see the world as God's creation. Only then do they realize their vocation and their destiny. Not in vain does the second Creation narrative say that man received life from the breath (Spirit) of God (Gen. 2:7). In biblical terms, the purpose of creation is to give and sustain life. The vocation of human beings is to live by the Spirit (breath) of God.

One of the characteristics of the Hellenistic Age was the widespread desire to ascend to the higher spheres of the chain of being and there participate in the activities of spiritual beings. The popular mystery religions promised its initiates journeys to the higher regions and knowledge of the mysteries of the universe. The Judaism of the time also encouraged ascents to the spiritual regions of the spheres by traveling on Elijah's chariot (2 Kings 2:11). To participate in such journeys through the spheres intense preparations were required. They included abstention from some activities and ascetic disciplines which helped the candidate get rid of earthly ballast. The letter *To the Colossians* is an argument against teachers who impose rules of "Do not handle, Do not taste, Do not [even] touch" (Col. 2:21), things that will prevent you from participating in "worship with angels and seeing hidden things" (Col. 2:18, my translation).

Initiates of the mystery cults fervently aspired to travel to the higher regions of the cosmos and went through the required disciplines to attain to the esoteric knowledge only available to those who had successful journeys. The Covenanters of Qumran had developed liturgies that, according to them, allowed participation in worship services with angels. We don't have enough information to know the circumstances and the motives informing Paul's trip to the third heaven (2 Cor. 12:2). Normally, those who had a successful trip through the spheres enjoyed great personal prestige. Paul, undoubtedly, had such a journey but refused the concomitant prestige. Still, his report of a successful journey through the spheres to Paradise itself is ample evidence of the high esteem in which these ascents were held. The desire to transcend the world of matter and soar to the higher spheres, the world of the Spirit, was very strong, indeed.

According to John considers such journeys irrelevant. With a few words it disqualifies them as real, emphatically stating: "No one has ascended into heaven" (3:13). Human beings on earth, however, can worship God "in Spirit," that is "in truth" (4:23), if they have been born of the Spirit who gives abundant life. There is no need to ascend to heaven to live in a spiritual creation.

The gospel's drama resides in this: he who descended and brought to the world life in the Spirit is about to return to the world above from whence he came. His departure could mean the end of all that the presence of the *Logos* in the flesh made available to human beings. Will it be possible to live successfully in the world below without the first *Parákletos* who makes "birth from above" possible? Are the disciples going to be left "desolate" (orphans, 14:18), abandoned to their own devices in the world below? Such an eventuality troubles the heart and leaves the disciples in despair (14:1).

The two farewell discourses of *According to John*, to a large degree, wish to explain that the return of the Son to the Father who sent him is no tragedy. This is a divine comedy. The drama of his mission in the world below has a happy ending. The departure of the Son does not put an end to the possibility for human beings to live in the Spirit. The divine initiative in the person of the Son is not coming to an end. Another *Parákletos* will take over his work so that life in the Spirit does not cease to be a reality among women and men. Jesus assures his disciples that his departure is to their advantage (16:7). They are uncertain of who Jesus is and do not grasp what he is accomplishing while incarnated among them. The other *Parákletos* to be sent by the Father at his request will make their uncertainty disappear (14:17). He is going to bear witness to Jesus (15:26). As it is now with Jesus (8:28; 12:50), so also will it be with the other *Parákletos,* who will say only what the Father tells him to say (16:13).

With a very laconic pronouncement the disciples are told that the *Parákletos* "will convince the world of sin, and of righteousness and of judgment" (16:8). He will convince of sin because he will make obvious the rejection of the Father in the person of the Son on the part of those who deny his claim to be the One Sent. Those who reject the Son are declared sinners (16:9). He will convince the world of God's righteousness by demonstrating that God is actually doing what is expected: God is making life in the Spirit available to all (16:10). The righteousness of God is fully evident when God's purposes are accomplished. He will convince of judgment because the successful completion of Jesus' mission and his glorification by the Father (12:28, 31) means that "the prince of this world" has been judged and stands condemned (16:11).

With these words the apocalyptic preoccupation with the elimination of evil and the vindication of the justice of God has been re-interpreted as already accomplished. The presence of the *Parákletos* among believers lifts them out of the world of sin and death. In this gospel Jesus gives the promise "I will come again" (14:3), but he does not go on to give an apocalyptic discourse about the return of the Son of Man in the clouds with a sickle in his hand. Astronomical disruptions, wars and rumors of wars, and a time of unprecedented troubles that culminate in a cataclysmic destruction of civilization are not featured in the symbolic universe of this gospel. There are no dramatic descriptions of the turning of the ages that bring about a new heaven and a new earth. The judgment of the world of sin has already taken place, and the believers already have eternal life. Those who keep his words "will never see death" (8:51). It is possible to live in the realm of the Spirit now.

The other *Parákletos*, the one who takes the place of the already glorified Son, also glorifies the Son, but not by receiving him victorious to the heavenly spheres from whence he had descended to the world below. He glorifies the Son by being the intermediary who conveys to those who belong to him the things that the Son wishes to give them (16:14). The Son is glorified by the permanent actualization of life in the Spirit by those living in the world below.

Jesus fulfills his promise to return and to send them the *Parákletos* the very Sunday of his resurrection. In the evening, when the worried and fearful disciples had closeted themselves with locked doors (20:19), Jesus appeared in their midst and breathing over them said: "Receive the Holy Spirit" (20:22), thus re-enacting God's gift of life to Adam. This is the creation of a new humanity. He has returned and fulfilled his promise to send them the Spirit. Born of the Spirit they live in him, and he is with them in the other *Parákletos*.

When Jesus promised to send his disciples the Spirit, he told them that the purpose for which he will send them this gift is to give them peace. Both farewell discourses close on this theme (14:27; 16:33). Life in the world below may have much tribulation, but the ones living "in the Spirit" live in the peace of Jesus. The peace of the Spirit, the peace of Jesus, is not like the peace of the world that is defined *via negativa* by the absence of war. The eschatological peace of the Spirit is defined by the abundance of life. God does not provide the Spirit "by measure" (3:34) to those born of the Spirit. God does not give it out carefully, according to a formula, stingily, taking care to save some for tomorrow. God gives it with an open hand, carelessly, prodigally. God squanders it without scruples and, as a consequence, those who receive it have abundant life in the Spirit. This is the new reality for those born "from above."

The gift, however, includes a discrete mission: to continue the work of the first *Parákletos*. The Spirit converts those begotten by him into agents of life. The Spirit and life are twins. The mission of the *Parákletos*, to engender life, is accomplished not only by the giving of life to those born of the Spirit, but when those born of the Spirit, as agents of eschatological peace, share their life with others. This is the ultimate will of the God who is Spirit (4:24). As children of the God who is Spirit, and who dispenses the Spirit freely, Christians are called upon to be agents of the peace and the joy that characterizes life in the Spirit. The abundant life that Jesus came to impart cannot be hoarded selfishly or shared stingily, "by measure." Christians cannot be but generous with their talents and disinterested with their lives. The God who creates them is prodigal by nature, and those who live in the Spirit, both in nature and in creation, cannot be otherwise.

14

REMEMBER MY WORDS

In 1901 Wilhelm Wrede shook the academic study of the gospels by arguing that not everything recorded in the gospel *According to Mark* had actually happened as described. In other words, the agenda of the writer was not to leave an account of what happened for the benefit of future generations, but to make faith in Jesus as the Christ reasonable and sustainable in light of his contemporary situation. The key for identifying his agenda is a *leitmotiv* that Wrede named "the messianic secret." It is present in the gospel in two basic forms or aspects.

In its most common aspect it shows Jesus imposing absolute silence on anyone who identifies him as the Son of God, or as the Christ, the Messiah. This is especially noticeable in the exorcisms: the unclean spirit dwelling in a poor human being identifies the exorcist before him. The narrator then says that "Jesus rebuked him, saying: 'Be silent'" (Mk. 1:25), or strictly commanded him to tell no one. This is also the case in the famous confession of Peter. When Peter says "You are the Christ," Jesus instructs all the disciples "to tell no one about him" (Mk. 8:30).

The other aspect of the messianic secret motif has Jesus explaining privately to a small group the significance of what he had told a crowd. Thus while the crowd is left wondering the meaning of what he had said, his disciples received inside information. He did this, for example, in the case of the parables of the kingdom, after having taught "a very large crowd" from a boat on the shore of the Sea of Galilee (Mk. 4:1). Later, "when he was alone [with] those who were about him with the twelve," Jesus starts his explication of the parables saying, "To you has been given the secret of the kingdom of God, but for those outside everything is in parables" (Mk. 4:10 – 11). The most striking example is the apocalyptic discourse. When he is in the temple before the crowds Jesus says, "Do you see these great buildings? There will not be left here one stone upon another that will not be thrown down." Later, on the Mount of Olives, Jesus expounds on the significance of his words to only four disciples: Peter, James, John and Andrew (Mk. 13:1 – 3). It is, no doubt, startling that the audience of what we call Jesus' apocalyptic discourse consisted of an extra-closed-inner-circle of four disciples.

The messianic secret, Wrede argued, is a literary device used by the narrator of *According to Mark* to explain how, after the resurrection, it had been possible for the disciples to proclaim Jesus as Messiah, the Christ. Many of their listeners, no doubt, had been acquainted with Jesus and knew what he had preached. During his ministry Jesus had not claimed to be the Messiah. There was, therefore, no reason for the disciples to assign this title to him after his crucifixion and resurrection. According to Wrede, the disciples responded to this objection by saying: "Jesus imposed silence on us about this back then, but privately he told us who he really was. Thus, even though there was no public recognition of Jesus as the Messiah during his ministry, we knew it all along."

Most scholars today recognize the messianic secret as a *leitmotiv* in *According to Mark* which was adopted by the other two synoptic gospels. Not many, however, agree to the explanation Wrede gave to its origin. Most recognize that the public ministry of Jesus must have had, at a minimum, messianic connotations. It is difficult to envision the Roman procurator ordering the crucifixion of Jesus if he did not have a messianic aura about him.

In *According to John* we find exactly the opposite to what Wrede described as the most common aspect of the messianic secret motif. Instead of imposing silence, Jesus proclaims to everyone within reach that he is the Son of God, the One Sent by the Father. From the very beginning Jesus is given titles that distinguish him from the rest of humanity. After having spent a day with Jesus, Andrew tells his brother Simon: "We have found the Messiah (which means Christ)" (1:41). John the Baptist twice makes the disclaimer "I am not the Christ" (1:20; 3:28), making clear in the process who is the Christ. When the Samaritan woman says to him: "I know that Messiah is coming (he who is called Christ)," Jesus tells her: "I who speak to you am he" (4:25 – 26). Later the Samaritans of Sychar confess: "We know that this is indeed the Savior of the world" (4:42). When the disciples are left wondering and confess: "This is a hard saying; who can listen to it?" (6:60), Jesus asks them if they intend to abandon him. The challenge makes them all confess: "We have believed and have come to know that you are the Holy One of God" (6:69). Hearing these confessions Jesus does not request any of their authors to keep them to themselves, as he does after the confession of Peter in the synoptics.

To the one born blind Jesus identifies himself as the Son of God (9:37). When those whom the narrator identifies as "the Jews" somewhat frustratedly insist: "If you are the Christ, tell us plainly," Jesus tells them: "I told you [already]" (10:24 – 25). When Martha confesses: "I believe that you are the Christ, the Son of God" (11:27), Jesus does not tell her to tell no one. Finally, when Pilate asks him about his disciples and his doctrine, Jesus assures him that his disciples had not received private instructions. He has taught only in public (18:20).

In *According to John,* it is clear, instead of imposing silence about his identity, Jesus openly proclaims it. In this way, this gospel negates one aspect of the messianic secret motif evident in the synoptics. The other aspect of the motif, however, is not negated, but modified. As noted above, in the synoptics during his ministry Jesus teaches the mystery of the kingdom of God to a small select group privately. In *According to John* understanding comes to the disciples through the "teaching" and the activation of memory by the Spirit after the resurrection. Or, as the disciples say when they hear the second farewell discourse: "Ah, now you are speaking plainly, not in any figure [of speech]! Now we know that you know all things ... by this we believe that you came from God" (16:29 – 30).

On several occasions throughout the gospel it is made clear that what Jesus is saying is not being understood by his hearers. Jesus insists that "at the beginning" he told everyone who he was (8:25), but his audience "did not understand that he spoke of the Father. So Jesus said, 'When you have lifted up the Son of man, then you will know that I am he'" (8:27 – 29). After he had drawn a contrast between the shepherd and the hirelings, the narrator explains: "This figure [of speech] Jesus used with them, but they did not understand what he was saying to them" (10:6).

After having supper with his disciples, Jesus began to wash their feet and Peter got upset saying: "Lord, do you wash my feet?" Jesus calmed him down saying: "What I am doing you do not know now, but afterward you will understand" (13:6 – 7). This explication does not apply only to the washing of the feet. It applies to the whole ministry of Jesus. The same explication is given by the narrator to the saying about the "rivers of living water" that will gush forth from Jesus' guts: "This he said about the Spirit, which those who believed in him would receive; for as yet the Spirit had not been given, because Jesus was not yet glorified" (7:39). In other words, at the time no one understood what Jesus had said. After his glorification at the cross and the reception of the Holy Spirit on resurrection Sunday the past was seen in a totally new light.

The clearest explication of the perspective from which these events are being narrated reads: "His disciples did not understand this at first; but when Jesus was glorified, then they remembered that this had been written of him and had been done to him" (12:16). And when Peter and the beloved disciple run to find out if it is true that Jesus' body had been stolen from the tomb and the door left open, the narrator explains that "as yet they did not know the scripture, that he must rise from the dead" (20:9).

Each gospel has a unique agenda, painting a picture of Jesus from a particular perspective which is aimed at a particular public. There is no question that the crucifixion left the disciples totally dumbfounded and the resurrection took them by surprise. Considering the significance of these two events the disciples eventually came to a quite different understanding of Jesus from the one they may have had during the time they were with him. *According to John* distinguishes itself by consciously admitting its vantage point. This, however, does not mean that this gospel is the only one with a vantage point from which to reconstruct the past and give its contemporaries a way to understand their experiences.

The full revelation of Jesus' identity and teachings was not within reach during his ministry. It became available only after his resurrection. In other words, the gospel *According to John,* like the synoptics, does not record what actually happened during the ministry of Jesus with the accuracy desired by modern historians. What we have is a presentation of the ministry of Jesus seen through the filter of theological reflection. As I have said in other meditations, those who read *According to John* must know the symbolic universe within which it works if they are going to understand it.

As a recounting of the life of Jesus, *According to John* does not give us enough information to write a biography. Since it was written in an oral culture years after the events had transpired, surely what is narrated depends on the collective memory of a community bound to the significance they give to the story. Memory, however, is not a modern electronic recorder; it selects, accommodates and interprets. To remember is not to preserve the past. It is to re-live it in the present. In this context, memory is the filter for theological reflection.

As Saint Augustine makes clear in his *Confessions*, faith lives in memory guided by the Holy Spirit. The role of memory as a guide must be taken into account when reading the gospel *According to John*. To their credit, the narrators openly admits being dependent on the benefit of memory. As a personal faculty, memory establishes identity for a person or community in time. The one who writes a *Memoir* does not write an autobiography. In it the author projects the image he wishes others to see, most probably with a central theme or specific trajectory that overlooks much. All four canonical gospels select and interpret past events to understand present experiences.

What had happened during the ministry of Jesus had not been understood by his disciples in the way in which it was understood after the resurrection by the collective memory informed by the Holy Spirit. Only after the glorification of the Son of man, his lifting up and returning to the Father, did his disciples "remember" the things that happened and understand that the Scriptures had predicted them. That is, the recognition of Jesus as the Savior of the world, the One Sent by the Father, came as the result of a memory that was energized after his glorification – a memory that "remembers" and interprets in light of the Scriptures guided by the Holy Spirit. In this gospel "remember" has a technical meaning. It is the mental function that, aided by the Holy Spirit, integrates the events in the life of Jesus to passages of the Scriptures that make them take new significance. As noted in a previous meditation, the references to time and feasts are really indicators of the meaning of what is being narrated.

We can then understand why the gospel says that Jesus, in his first farewell discourse, promised his disciples that the function of the Parákletos was to "remind" them of what Jesus had said when he was with them. "But the Counselor, the Holy Spirit, whom the Father will send in my name, he will teach you all things, and bring to your remembrance all that I have said to you" (14:26). This promise is preceded by the explanation: "These things I have spoken to you while I am still with you" (14:25). But in the second farewell discourse Jesus tells his disciples: "I have said these things to you, that when their hour comes you may remember that I have told you of them. I did not say these things to you from the beginning, because I was with you" (16:4). How are we to understand this?

It would seem that the one speaking in the second discourse is the Risen Christ, not the Jesus who was yet to be crucified. Are we to understand that Jesus told them about "these things … from the beginning," when he was with them, or that he did not tell them about these things precisely because he was with them? If he did not tell them because he was with them, how was it going to be possible for them to "remember" what he did not tell them? Or, is it that the Holy Spirit is going to "teach" them and "remind" them of what Jesus did not tell them when he was with them at the beginning? This rather convoluted explanation is an admission that the gospel is serving as the guide which the Johannine community has for making sense of their Christian experiences. Whatever the circumstances they face they find meaning for them "remembering" how the Scriptures shed light on the life of Jesus.

The roots for the use of memory as a theological faculty, which does not limit itself to retaining something in the mind but also informs action, are found in the Old Testament. In his discourse to the people before entering into Canaan Moses tells them: "Take heed and keep your soul diligently, lest you forget the things which your eyes have seen" (Dt. 4:9, cp. 4:23, 6:12). Micah transmits the word of the Lord: "O my people, remember … that you may know the saving acts of the Lord" (Mic. 6:5). In a psalm recorded in 1 Chronicles, David sings: "Remember the wonderful works he has done, the wonders he wrought, the judgments he uttered" (1Chr. 16:12). After a brief summary of the *magnalia dei* done on behalf of the people, Nehemiah laments: "they refused to obey and forgot the wonders which thou didst perform" (Neh. 9:17). Whereas the fourth commandment in Deuteronomy begins by saying: "Observe the sabbath day, to keep it holy" (Dt. 5:12), the same command in Exodus reads: "Remember the sabbath day, to keep it holy" (Ex. 20:8). To remember, not to forget, is to behave obediently with full understanding of what is required, keeping in mind the mighty acts of God.

The gospel *According to John* pronounces a beatitude on those who have not seen and yet believed (20:29). This applies to all those who confess: "We believe that you came from God." All future generations of believers are contemporaries of Jesus who can remember his mighty deeds because the Comforter, the Spirit of Truth, teaches them and "re-minds" them of what they have neither seen nor heard. Once the disciples received the Holy Spirit who taught them all things and reminded them of all things in the light of the Scriptures, then and only then did they understand what Jesus had been about. This is the Johannine definition of the memory that is guided by the Holy Spirit. It understands what it did not know and remembers what it had neither seen nor heard in order to actualize in labors of love the life of Jesus on earth. To all his disciples Jesus says: "Remember the word that I said to you" (15:20). His word will allow you to understand what you are experiencing. The Christian life consists in actualizing what is remembered about the Son sent by the Father.

15

SALVATION IS FROM THE JEWS

It is impossible to read *According to John* and not become aware of its dependence on the Scriptures, the Torah. In the same way in which it is taken for granted that the reader knows its content before beginning to read, it is also assumed that the reader knows well the stories of the patriarchs and the books of the prophets and the Psalms. It is only under the light of the Scriptures that the life of Jesus can be understood.

For example, the image of the good shepherd (10:1 – 18) is a re-application of the reference to the shepherds of Israel that Ezekiel forcefully denounces (Ez. 34:1 – 10). Due to the failure of the shepherds to whom God had entrusted the flock, God promises to become its shepherd from then on (Ez. 11 – 16). This promise, the gospel tells us, is being fulfilled in the person of Jesus.

The narrative of Jesus' encounter with the Samaritan woman echoes the story of the encounter of Eliezer with Rebekah (Gen. 24:11 – 61). In both stories someone is at a well and in need of help. After a young woman provides the needed help and talks with the stranger she decides to go home to tell her folks what happened at the well. Thus, the local men come out to meet the stranger and invite him to stay with them. Once the stranger enjoys the hospitality that has been offered, he explains his mission, and the local people respond positively. Obviously, those who told the story of the Samaritan woman recognized that what had taken place was already written in the Scriptures, and recognized the similarity as a significant clue of God's present plans.

It is not difficult to see the parallels between Nathanael, the true Israelite who sat under a fig tree and in whom there is no guile (1:47), and Jacob, the one who by guile took the birthright from his brother Esau and had to flee the paternal home. Running from the angry brother who seeks vengeance, Jacob spends the night sleeping in the desert with a rock for a pillow. That night he dreams of a ladder that reaches from heaven down to the very spot in which he sleeps. On it angels descend and ascend, making possible the exchange of offerings and gifts between two unbridgeable realms. When Jacob wakes up in the morning he builds an altar, and Beth-el becomes a worship center for his descendants.

To Nathanael, the one who lives protected and nourished by the family's Israelite traditions (the fig tree), Jesus promises a vision that surpasses Jacob's dream by far. He is going to see the heavens open and the angels who descend and ascend upon the Son of Man. Jacob's ladder has been displaced by the Son of Man on a cross, the instrument of his ascension. He is the one who opens the lines of communication between earth and heaven. The true Israelites are those who see and believe in the Son of Man, but to understand this it is necessary to know the story of Jacob, the deceiver, whose name was later changed to Israel.

In my previous meditation I pointed out that the gospel is not a factual account of what took place, but the result of theological reflection on what took place by a community that "remembers" the past in the light of the Scriptures and the "teaching" of the Comforter (14:26). I also pointed out that the understanding of memory as a theological faculty has its roots in the Scriptures. Even though *According to John* does not quote the Old Testament as frequently as the other gospels and does not, like *According to Matthew*, claim repeatedly that what is being narrated is the fulfillment of a specific prophecy, it is the gospel most firmly rooted in the traditions of the Old Testament.

In his conversation with the Samaritan woman, Jesus tells her: "Salvation is from the Jews" (4:22). With these words the Jews are placed at the very core of God's will to give life to humanity. The agency of the Jews as the chosen nation in history is essential to the divine purpose. In its immediate context this declaration privileges the Jews and leaves in limbo the Samaritans who are put down for worshiping what they know not (4:22). However, given the context, the declaration that privileges the Jews as the agents of salvation is somewhat diluted by the declaration that both the worship on Mount Gerizim, based on ignorance, and the worship on Mount Zion, based on knowledge, have been displaced by the worship of the Father "in Spirit and in truth" (4:23).

The symbolic universe of *According to John* is built on the revelation of God found in the Scriptures. There the Jews are identified as the people chosen by God as the agents of salvation for all the nations. It is, therefore, surprising to find that throughout the gospel "the Jews" are identified as the agents of their "father the Devil," who operates on the basis of lies (8:44). The Law is derogatorily put down as "your law" (10:34; 15:25; 18:31), and "the Jews" own it as "our law" (7:51; 19:7). With characteristic Johannine irony, "the Jews" say: "We know God has spoken to Moses, but as for this man, we do not know where he comes from" (9:29). Moses is shown at a marked disadvantage by negative comparisons with Jesus. The one brought in the law, while the other personifies grace and truth (1:18). The one is a District Attorney who accuses (5:41), while the other is the Son or Man who gives life (10:10). The disciples of Moses (9:28) are blind (9:41), while those of Jesus see (9:37 – 38).

Among the first Christians there must have been Samaritans and "Greeks," that is gentiles, but the majority of them, without a doubt, were Jews. The gospel recognizes that many Jews believed in Jesus (7:31; 8:31; 11:45; 12:11, 42), but these believers are overshadowed by the repeated references to "the Jews" who wished to kill him, especially the princes, priests and Pharisees (5:16, 18; 7:1, 25, 30; 8:40, 59; 10:31). All these references belong to a time during Jesus' ministry that is well before his passion. The resurrection of Lazarus is the last drop making the glass overflow, and "the Jews" decide not only to kill Jesus (11:53) but also Lazarus (12:10).

The Jews of the time of Jesus did not distinguish themselves by being one monolithic block of people. Among them there were Sadducees, Pharisees, Essenes, Nazarenes, Herodians, Therapeutai, Zealots, Sicarii, Covenanters, *am ha aretz*, etc. With the exception of the Covenanters (of Qumran and other localities), who organized themselves in sectarian communities in opposition to the temple hierarchy, and the *am ha aretz*, the irreligious populace, all Jews had two things in common: their adherence to the temple of Jerusalem and their dependence on the Pentateuch as Scripture. *The Acts of the Apostles* makes clear that Christians continued to participate in the services of the temple and the annual feasts of Judaism after the resurrection of Christ.

This situation changed radically with the destruction of the temple in 70 CE. The only Jews able to survive without the temple of Jerusalem were the Christians and the Pharisees, and to do it they had to forge institutions with new identities.

The Pharisees gave new importance to the Scribes and the Rabbis as interpreters of the law and constituted the Council of Jamnia to start the process that brought forth the Mishna toward the end of the second century, and centuries later the Talmud. This council also established the canon of Tanakh, what Christians call the Old Testament, and began the process that established the order of services at the synagogue. Eventually the synagogues became centers of worship with the ark of the covenant containing the rolls of Tanakh as the focus of attention. Archaeologists have not found synagogues with arks for the Torah scrolls prior to 250 CE. It took time to determine that an alternative to the temple needed to be established.

The Bar Kochbah revolt (132-135 CE) which enjoyed the support of Rabbi Akiba, one of the most prominent rabbis of the time, put an end to the hopes harbored by many who wished to re-establish official services at the temple. There is evidence indicating that between the years 70 and 135 Jews made pilgrimages to Jerusalem to offer sacrifices at the ruins of the altar. In 135 the Romans converted Jerusalem into a Roman colony and named it Aelia Capitolina. *According to John* tells us that the destruction of the temple means the collapse of a cosmology. The new temple is the body of the Risen One, and true worship is now rendered "in Spirit and in truth" rather than upon an altar.

The Council of Jamnia brought about the institutionalization of Pharisaism and established the parameters of the identity of Rabbinic Judaism. The Eighteen Benedictions became part of the services at the synagogues. One of these "benedictions" pronounced a curse on Christians. No doubt the references to "expulsion from the synagogue" (9:22, 34; 12:42; 16:2), and to "fear of the Jews" (7:13, 19; 19:38; 20:19) refer to the situation the Johannine community was confronting when the gospel was in the last stages of its redactional process toward the end of the first century. This situation caused some to be "secret" disciples (20:19), and others to avoid compromising questions (9:22); it explains the negative references to the Mosaic law and Moses' disciples, as well as to "the Jews" as unbelievers who reject the revelation of Jesus as the One Sent to bring life to the world.

With the destruction of the Jerusalem temple, the Judaism of Jesus' time ceased to exist. This means that the references to "the Jews" in *According to John* in reality identify the members of the Rabbinic synagogues that emerged toward the end of the first century. Rabbinic Judaism and the early Christian movement were at that time engaged in a ferocious fight to be recognized as the one legitimate heir of the wealth of their dead mother, the religion centered on the temple of Jerusalem. Their battle was primarily concerned with the authority to be the true interpreter of the Law and the Prophets. The rabbis produced the *haggada* and the *halacha*. The first was intended to foster the life of devotion by highlighting the spiritual meanings of the biblical stories. The second was intended to apply the laws of the Pentateuch to the life situations encountered in Hellenistic urban contexts. Christians, for their part, continued their use of the Scriptures to give form and content to their understanding of the life and death of Jesus as the One Sent by the Father to give life to the world.

This fight is given dramatic heights in chapters 7 and 8 of *According to John* where the desire to kill Jesus underlines the narratives. From the beginning Jesus is accused of being possessed by a demon (7:20). Then reasons are given as to why his claim to be sent by God is incredible. Since it is known where he is from (irony), he cannot be the Christ (7:27). He is a Galilean; therefore, he cannot be the Christ (7:41, 52). No one with authority has believed his claim; therefore, he can be ignored (7:48). He is the only one claiming to be what he obviously is not (8:13).

These disqualifications are followed by a characterization that must have had its origin in the first century and eventually became standard in the Talmud: Jesus is a bastard, a son without a known father. The question is: "Where is your father?" (8:19). In other words, "Who are you?" (8:25). For their part, "the Jews" claim: "We are descendants of Abraham, and have never been in bondage to any one" (8:33). Jesus grants them their claim: "I know that you are descendants of Abraham, yet you seek to kill me" (8:37). This means that you are servants of sin (8:34) and that you will die in your sins (8:24). At this "the Jews" put out their ultimate insult and make their ultimate claim: "We were not born of fornication [like you]; we have one father, even God." To this accusation Jesus answers: "You are of your father the devil…you are not of God" (8:44, 47).

The dialogue has descended where arguments are absent and insults take their place. "The Jews" then say: "Are we not right in saying that you are a Samaritan and have a demon?" (8:48). It is remarkable that after calling Jesus a bastard born out of fornication, which contradicts their argument that he cannot be the Messiah because his father and mother are well known by all (6:42), they accuse him of being a Samaritan, apparently an even worse insult.

That the Jews and the Samaritans did not enjoy each other's company and harbored strong prejudices against each other is amply demonstrated by both Jewish and Samaritan literature. It must be noted, however, that in many ways Samaritanism was just another one of the many varieties of Judaism in existence in the first century. Political, social and economic tensions between the North and the South of Israel can be traced back to the time of the judges, before the establishment of the Davidic dynasty in the tenth century BCE. These tensions, of course, also involved religious concerns about sacred sites. The serious animosities that characterized Jew-Samaritan relations did not flare up until the establishment of the Hasmonean dynasty after the Maccabean War (167 – 164 BCE). As a sacred spot with cosmic significance, Mount Gerizim had deeper roots in the religious traditions of the land than Mount Zion, which had been a threshing floor before the temple was built on it (2 Sam. 24:16 – 25; 1 Chron. 21:18 – 22:1). The destruction of the temple on Mount Gerizim in 127 BCE and of the city of Samaria in 109 BCE by John Hyrcanus were traumatic events that left ugly scars exposed and in need of constant attention. It is quite telling, indeed, and quite ironic, that in a community that counted Samaritans among its members it was said that the ultimate insult "the Jews" could hurl at Jesus was that he was a Samaritan possessed by a demon. Apparently a bastard could be looked down upon and despised, but a Samaritan could be safely ignored.

Unfortunately, the vitriolic polemic between "the Jews" and Christians of the latter part of the first century created the conditions that inform the history of these two communities during the next twenty centuries, a history that reached its climax in the Holocaust. A poorly informed reading of the gospels *According to Matthew* and *According to John*, where this anti-Judaic (not anti-Semitic) animosity is on the surface, is to a large extent responsible for this tragic history. It is high time for all Christians to recognize the origin of this animosity and thereby learn to live with their cousins who also believe in the God of Abraham, Isaac and Jacob. Knowledge of history is the best antidote against bad behavior. Ignorance may condemn one to repeat past mistakes. Misconstructions of history many times serve to promote abuses of power. An honest look at history should promote understanding and the vision with which to chart new directions for the future. The God of Abraham, Isaac and Jacob is not just the God of Jews, Samaritans and Christians. He is also the God of Islam. Putting an end to the battle for the inheritance of the mother that was buried at the destruction of the Second Temple on the part of those who insist on the monotheistic worship of God is still a goal to be achieved. These animosities, unfortunately, many times serve well people with political agendas, but their eradication should be a high priority for all those who recognize their origin and aim to bring peace among all the children of God.

16

DID I NOT CHOOSE YOU, THE TWELVE?

The calling of the twelve disciples and their significant role in the life of Jesus is one of the prominent features in the stories of the gospels. *According to Mark* stops the narrative to give a list of the men Jesus set apart. It begins with two sets of brothers, Simon and Andrew from Bethsaida and the sons of Zebedee: James and John. It then lists Philip, Bartholomew, Matthew, Thomas, James son of Alphaeus, Thaddeus, Simon the Cananaean, and Judas Iscariot. It also says that Jesus gave to Simon the surname Peter and to James and John that of Sons of Thunder. Judas Iscariot is identified as he "who betrayed him." Their appointment was "to be with him, to be sent to preach and to have authority over demons" (Mk. 3:14 – 19).

According to Matthew gives exactly the same list and expands the healing mission so that the twelve would not only have "authority over unclean spirits, to cast them out" but also the ability "to heal every disease and every infirmity." It does not mention their mission to preach (Mt. 10:1 – 4). *According to Luke* introduces some changes in the list. Instead of Simon the Cananaean it names a Simon the Zealot. It is not clear that the two descriptions belong to the same man since Simon was a popular name. Instead of Thaddeus, it lists Judas son of James and explains that these twelve were named "apostles" (Lk. 6:12 – 16). This gospel is the first of a two-volume work that emphasizes the expansion of Christianity within the Roman empire and tones down the strong apocalyptic outlook of *According to Mark*, it is understandable that it transforms the disciples into apostles and overlooks their authority to overpower the forces of evil by casting out demons.

The picture of the twelve in *According to Mark* is somewhat puzzling. Jesus often gives them special private instruction (Mk. 4:10, 34; 9:35; 10:32; 12:43; 13:3; 14:33), but even more often the narrator points out that they did not understand what Jesus had said (Mk. 6:52; 8:17 – 18, 21, 29; 9:18, 32; 10:10, 23, 26, 38). With noticeable frustration Jesus asks them: "Are your hearts hardened?" (8:17). The narrative highlights their lack of understanding pointing out that when Peter insists that if necessary he would die with Jesus rather than deny him, the reader is told that "they all said the same" (Mk. 14:31). Just a few verses later the narrator pointedly records that "they all forsook him and fled" (Mk. 14:50).

Also prominent in *According to Mark* is the characterization of the disciples as fearful rather than faithful (4:40; 5:15, 36; 6:50; 9:6, 32). The earliest manuscripts of this gospel end in 16:8. This ending is rather abrupt and intriguing. It tells that the women who had discovered the empty tomb and had been ordered to go and inform the disciples that Jesus would meet them in Galilee, left the tomb "and said nothing to any one, because they were afraid" (Mk. 16:8). Today most scholars believe that in fact that was the original ending. It emphasizes the characterization of the disciples as fearful rather than obedient.

Another feature of this gospel is the request on the part of James and John to have Jesus do whatever they would ask of him, specifically, in the first instance, to have them sit to his right and left side when he would reign in glory (Mk. 10:35). This presumptuous request for privilege got from Jesus a reality check that pointed out the responsibilities of discipleship (Mk. 10:38) and caused the other ten disciples to become indignant with the two who demanded special honors (Mk. 10:41). The moral of this story is given by Jesus' instructions in the verses following: In worldly organizations some assume roles that allow them to rule over the rest. It shall not be this way among the disciples of Jesus. Most students of *According to Mark* see here an argument on the part of Markan Christianity to put down the original disciples and to reject the creation of an ecclesiastical hierarchy within an institutionalized Christianity.

The gospel *According to John* departs from the synoptic tradition by not giving a list of the twelve disciples. It makes references to the disciples frequently through the story, and it does know of the twelve (6:70 – 71). Quite often, however, it highlights specific disciples. In *According to Mark*, some disciples are also highlighted. Peter is given a prominent role (Mk. 8:29; 10:28; 11:21; 14:31, 37, 54, 72; 16:7). Moreover, the two sets of brothers, Peter and Andrew, James and John, are the only hearers of the apocalyptic discourse (13:3), and the trio of Peter, James and John is the one taken deeper into the garden of Gethsemane to pray with Jesus (14:33). Judas Iscariot, the one who betrayed him, is twice identified as "one of the twelve" (Mk. 14:10, 43). Besides these references to particular disciples, there is only one occasion where a disciple is singled out. John informs Jesus that they had seen a man casting out demons, and they had forbidden him to do it because he was not a follower of Jesus (Mk. 9:38)

According to John gives Andrew, Peter, Philip, Nathanael , Thomas , Judas Iscariot, Judas (not Iscariot) and an unnamed disciple important parts in the story. Nathanael does not appear in the synoptic lists; Judas (not Iscariot) is most likely the one identified in *According to Luke* as Judas son of James, but is unknown to *According to Mark* and *According to Matthew*. This gospel also has intriguing references to "the disciple whom Jesus loved." All in all, it is apparent that *According to John* sees the disciples through a different set of glasses than do the synoptics.

That Jesus had twelve disciples is mentioned only when Judas is identified as the traitor (6:70 – 71). The synoptics include Judas Iscariot as one of the twelve in their lists. These references to Judas are the most powerful evidence to establish the historical existence of the close circle of twelve disciples. Among those who try to reconstruct what can be said about Jesus with the certainty gained using the methodologies normally used by historians, quite a few have doubted that Jesus actually chose a group of twelve who stayed with him throughout his ministry. According to them, the early Christians created the notion of a circle of twelve disciples in an effort to establish the authenticity of their new religion as a substitute for the religion of Israel. These became the twelve apostles on whom the church was built — as a counterpart to the twelve patriarchs, the progenitors of the twelve tribes of Israel. Using the same model, the editors of the Torah had earlier created the collection of the twelve minor prophets.

The consistent identification of Judas Iscariot as one of the twelve disciples makes it very unlikely that the circle of the twelve was invented by early Christians seeking to build the church on a patriarchal foundation. If they had been creating a fictitious group as the foundation of the church they would not have made a robber and a traitor a member of it. On the other hand, it is quite likely that one who came preaching that the kingdom of heaven is at hand would have formed a group of twelve disciples to anticipate and to announce the restoration of Israel. That one of the twelve would then act treasonously on the basis of misguided apocalyptic notions or some other reason is well within what historians would consider probable. Besides, it is unlikely that as early as the gospel *According to Mark*, the first of the gospels to be written, both the fiction of a circle of twelve disciples and an argument against them as a privileged group would have been created.

In *According to John* it is also pointed out that many times the disciples did not understand the significance of what Jesus had said or done. Later, with the aid of the Holy Spirit given to them when Jesus appeared on resurrection Sunday and in the light of definite passages of Scripture, they "remembered" what had happened or had been said in a totally different light. This gospel records (unlike the synoptics) that as witnesses of the first sign, the changing of water into vine at a wedding feast, "they believed in him" (2:11). At the discourse about the bread that descended from heaven, when Jesus says that it is necessary to eat the flesh and drink the blood of the Son of man, "many of his disciples, when they heard that, said, 'This is a hard saying, who can listen to it?'" (6:60). Those disciples who found this hard to take, the narrator says, "no longer went about with him" (6:66). Then Jesus turned specifically to the twelve and asked them: "Do you also wish to go away?" Simon Peter took the initiative and spoke for the twelve: "Lord, to whom shall we go? You have the words of eternal life, and we have believed, and have come to know, that you are the Holy One of God" (6:68 – 69). This incident makes clear that the twelve were distinguished from other "disciples" who also followed Jesus.

The Johannine confession of Peter is the counterpart to Peter's confession recorded in *According to Mark*, where he says: "You are the Christ," in answer to the question, "Who do you say that I am?" (Mk. 8:29). As noted in a previous meditation, the title Christ is not considered adequate by the Johannine community. The title Holy One of God is found only here. This was, no doubt, Peter's best hour. *According to John* does not report the agony of Jesus in the garden in the Kidron valley when Peter, James and John fell asleep rather than praying with him. Neither does it report that when Jesus was taken prisoner by the soldiers the disciples forsook him and fled (Mk. 14:50). Peter's portrait, however, is enriched by his refusal to have Jesus wash his feet, and then pleading with him to wash not just his feet but his whole body (13:6 – 9). He is the one who asks how Jesus could possibly go to a place where he could not follow him (13:36 – 37). He also cut the ear off a servant of the High Priest in the garden when the soldiers were taking Jesus away (18:10). These incidents point out that in spite of the moment of illumination that caused him to declare Jesus the Holy One of God, he had not fully understood the mission Jesus had been sent to accomplish.

Throughout the gospel *According to John* other disciples are given cameo roles. Andrew is the one who informs Jesus that he had seen a lad with five barley loaves and two fishes (6:8). He is also the one who, together with Philip, tells Jesus that some Greeks wish to see him (12:23). Philip is the one who was approached by the Greeks and then approached Andrew with their request (12:23). Judas (not Iscariot) is the one who asks Jesus a question that foreshadows his post resurrection appearances to his disciples: "Lord, how is it that you will manifest yourself to us, and not to the world?" (14:22). Jesus' answer describes those who love him as those who keep his word. In other words, Judas is told that true disciples trust his word.

Thomas the Twin, plays a significant role in two crucial incidents. After Jesus' polemical encounter with "the Jews" in chapters seven to ten, during which on more than one occasion "the Jews" tried to kill him, Jesus took refuge on the other side of the Jordan where he and John the Baptist had once been baptizing. There Jesus received word that Lazarus was ill. Eventually, Jesus responded to the news saying: "Let us go unto Judea again" (11:7). The disciples then alerted Jesus of the danger involved, but Jesus insisted, saying: "Let us go to him" (11:15). Now Thomas said to his colleagues, "Let us also go, that we may die with him" (11:16). His effort to convince the others to go with Jesus to Judea again, even if it meant dying with him, it would appear, was quite appropriate as a demonstration of loyalty. Still, we may relish the irony of the situation. Jesus is not going to Bethany to die. He has already said that Lazarus' illness is not unto death. "It is for the glory of God, so that the Son of God may be glorified by means of it" (11:4). In fact he is going to Judea again to exercise the power to give life. Thomas' resolve is laudable, but misinformed. Its ironic twist serves to highlight what is really going to happen.

Thomas the Twin, is also the one who was absent from the upper room on resurrection Sunday, but was there the following Sunday. To him Jesus appeared specifically to show him the marks of the nails in his hand and the wound made by the lance in his side. Given that the evidence forces him to deny his former skepticism, Thomas pronounces the confession that all readers of this gospel are expected to make: "My Lord and my God" (20:28). But the appearance necessitated by Thomas' skepticism, undoubtedly aimed against a docetic understanding of the Risen Lord, immediately gets qualified. Those who will in the future confess "my God" need not see and touch what Thomas saw and touched.

Finally, we may note the listing of the disciples who went back to fishing on the Sea of Galilee. The group is made up of Simon Peter, Thomas the Twin, Nathanael of Cana of Galilee, the sons of Zebedee, and two other disciples (21:2). Here we have seven disciples, rather than twelve. The first three we have met before. There is no way to know who "the two other disciples" were, and we have not met "the sons of Zebedee" in this gospel before, neither as sons of Zebedee nor as James and John. It would appear, therefore, that the identity of the sons of Zebedee was part of the oral tradition known to the Johannine community.

Since the gospel has an ending in verses thirty and thirty one of chapter twenty, it is reasonable to think that chapter twenty one was added to the gospel at a later time. The obvious question is, Why? Most likely, it was added for two reasons: first, to incorporate the Johannine community, which had developed on the fringes of the Christian movement, into the mainstream where Peter and James were leading figures; and second, to point out that it was not true that the founder of the community was not supposed to die, as apparently members of the community believed at one time (21:23).

In this chapter, the Living Christ serves seven disciples the same kind of food he had once used to feed five thousand. He also causes these disciples to catch 153 large fishes (21:11). This miraculous catch consists of a perfect number, like the 144,000 of *Revelation* (Rev. 7:4). The number is the triangular of $10 + 7 = 17$. If one adds the sequence of numbers beginning with 1 and ending with 17, the sum is 153. Thus, this chapter gives its approval to the church as a perfect institution and appoints Peter, the one who pledged to die before he would deny his Lord but actually denied him three times, as the pastor of the flock. Besides, it acknowledges his death as a martyr (21:15 – 19).

Chapter 21 also clarifies that "the disciple whom Jesus loved," who apparently by the time this chapter was added had already died, had not been singled out by Jesus as one who would remain alive until he came (21:22 – 23). This mysterious disciple has traditionally been identified as John the son of Zebedee. Other identifications have also been suggested. One of the more likely among them is that he is Lazarus. The suggestion is based on the form in which the news of his illness comes to Jesus: "Lord, he whom you love is ill" (11:3). It is also significant that Lazarus is mentioned to have been present at the anointing, the anticipation of his burial, and that "the Jews" decided to kill him as well as Jesus (12:1, 9 – 10). The fact that the disciple whom Jesus loved is among the seven fishing in the Sea of Galilee and the group includes John and James, the two sons of Zebedee, makes it possible to identify the beloved disciple as John (21:2, 7). On the other hand, when disciples are mentioned they are consistently given an identification mark. Simon is the one Jesus named Peter. Thomas is the Twin. Andrew is the brother of Peter, Philip is from Bethsaida, the city of Peter and Andrew, Nathanael is from Cana in Galilee, and Judas is Iscariot or the son of Simon Iscariot (13:26). The other Judas is not Iscariot. Nicodemus is the one who came to Jesus by night. Joseph of Arimathea is a secret disciple. Martha is Mary's sister. Mary is the one who anointed the Lord with ointment and wiped his feet with her hair (11:2). If John is "the disciple whom Jesus loved" we are justified in expecting the pattern to appear also in this case, but it does not. It is, therefore, quite probable that "the disciple whom Jesus loved" is one of "the two other disciples" who remained unidentified and were among the seven who went fishing. This would account for the inclusion of two unidentified disciples in the group that went fishing, particularly if the founder of the community was not one of the twelve.

The suggestion made by Raymond E. Brown, therefore, is the best available: the "disciple whom Jesus loved" is the founder of the Johannine community who is credited with certifying the truth of the gospel at the end of chapter twenty one, but may not have been one of the twelve. He was the one known to love Jesus singularly and to be one whom Jesus loved.

Most scholars today admit that all the canonical gospels were written anonymously. The titles ascribing them to prominent persons among the early Christians (as *According to Matthew*, etc.)

were assigned when they began to circulate together in the second century. This was part of the process that brought about the institutionalization of Christianity. The Jesus movement, composed of disciples who accompanied him during his lifetime, became several movements about the Living Christ after Jesus' crucifixion. By the end of the first century these different organisms were being conformed into an organization.

This means that the title of the gospel *According to John* does not belong together with the credit given to "the disciple whom Jesus loved" as the one who certifies its authenticity. Still, in this gospel the disciples play a most significant role as dialogue partners with Jesus, and their faith is duly recognized. The mostly negative picture of the disciples that characterizes *According to Mark*, which is softened but still present in the other two synoptics, is absent in *According to John.* In it the disciples are significant partners who play important roles in the presentation of Jesus' mission, even when their words are coated with irony. Most significantly, they serve as prototypes of all the future disciples who would not see Jesus but would believe in him as the One Sent by the Father.

17

The House was Filled with the Fragrance of Her Ointment

It is somewhat surprising that in a gospel that sees the incarnation at the core of God's work of salvation, there is no account or recognition of the circumstances surrounding the birth of Jesus from a woman. Jesus' mother, who is repeatedly featured in the story, is not mentioned by name. This is even more surprising in a gospel where women are given especially prominent roles.

According to Mark also does not mention Jesus' birth, and seems to indicate that Jesus was adopted as the Son of God at his baptism. Throughout this gospel Jesus is presented as a man who has been commissioned by God to pay the ransom for the sins of human beings (Mk. 10:45). *According to Matthew* and *According to Luke*, on their part, narrate the birth produced by the Holy Spirit and a young woman (Mt. 1:20; Lk. 1:35). The baby born of Mary is divine because his father is the Holy Spirit. These gospels tell the story of his birth from quite different points of view, but both point out that Mary was impregnated by the Holy Spirit. Her child was not just another human being. It is surprising, therefore, that in these two gospels Mary does not play other significant roles during the ministry of Jesus.

The three synoptic gospels say that on one occasion the disciples advised Jesus that his mother and brothers wished to talk with him, but the multitude was preventing them from getting close. On this occasion, when he had the opportunity to re-establish a connection with his family, Jesus ignored his closest relatives and declared that his family consists of those who do the will of God (Mk. 3:31 – 34; Mt. 12:46 – 50; Lk. 8:19 – 21).

In *According to John*, as already stated, nothing is said about Jesus' birth. What counts is that the *Logos* became flesh. Reading this gospel we do not learn that his mother was called Mary. The Holy Spirit, who without a doubt plays a major role in the gospel, has nothing to do with his coming to the world. John the Baptist is the only one who sees the Holy Spirit descend on Jesus and testifies to that effect (1:32). The incarnation here does not involve a miraculous birth, but the mother of Jesus, who remains anonymous, plays a prominent role in the first sign performed by Jesus and in the sign that is the anti-type of all the signs, the crucifixion.

In *According to John* the mother of Jesus is not an innocent and submissive young woman. At the wedding feast in Cana she is the one who is aware of what is taking place and alerts Jesus of the situation. The hosts have run out of wine, and their feast is in danger of ending in a fiasco. Jesus' sharp reply to his mother must be understood in the context in which all the dialogues of Jesus are presented in this gospel. Whoever starts a conversation with Jesus receives a sharp answer and ends up looking bad or ignored. Be it Nicodemus, the Samaritan woman, Mary and Martha of Bethany, the Greeks, Peter, Nathanael, Philip, or Jesus' mother, they all need to take a second look and adopt a new perspective. This makes one suspect that the redactors of the gospel have used these interlocutors to develop their own agenda.

Be that as it may, at the wedding feast in Cana Jesus' mother and his brothers are at the celebration, and his mother is involved with the activities that promote the well-being of those in attendance. While helping with the things that make friends, neighbors and relatives feel that the spirit of confraternity unites them and gives them joy, Jesus' mother becomes aware there is no more wine and gives Jesus the news. What distinguishes her is that she does not take Jesus' dismissive comment as a negative answer. She demonstrates her faith by telling the servants to fulfill faithfully whatever Jesus orders. She is confident that, given the situation, Jesus will act. She sees beyond Jesus' sharp comment to his sense of duty. She is the only one at the very beginning of his ministry who has a glimmer that Jesus can provide the wine that the feast requires. Mary's intervention foretells the purpose of Jesus' presence among humans.

Only in *According to John* do we learn that Jesus spent two days in Sychar and that, as a result of his stay there, many of the inhabitants of the city came to believe in him. This amazing success was made possible by the testimony of a woman. When she saw herself exposed, instead of taking offense, she thought that the one talking with her might be the prophet the Samaritans were waiting for. Her life, like that of all humans, had had its ups and downs, but at the crucial moment, when she faced the Son of God, she did what the occasion required. When her "hour" came, she acted decisively. Forgetting the purpose for which she had gone to the well, she left her jar behind and ran to announce that the prophet promised by Moses was a short distance away. In response, the people of the town came out to see the stranger, and they invited him to stay with them. When two days later Jesus departed, the townspeople said to the woman: "It is no longer because of your words that we believe, for we have heard for ourselves, and we know that this is indeed the Savior of the world" (4:42). Thus the testimony of the Samaritan woman was confirmed and expanded.

The anecdote of the woman accused of adultery and about to be stoned by the Scribes and the Pharisees obviously circulated freely in the oral tradition of the early Christians. The oldest New Testament manuscripts do not contain this pericope at the beginning of chapter eight of *According to John*. The story does appear attached to the end of this gospel in several manuscripts. One manuscript has this story after 21:38 in *According to Luke*. The position it occupies in our modern Bibles is the one found in late manuscripts, but it interrupts the virulent controversy going on between Jesus and "the Jews" in chapters 7 and 8. In any case, as part of the oral tradition, it undoubtedly preserves a dramatic life situation and an important lesson.

The anecdote offers a radical criticism of the hypocrisy of a misogynist culture. Instead of identifying with the judges who impose the law, Jesus identifies himself with the ones who hear the voice of their conscience and recognize that it is stronger than that of the law. The law, no doubt, condemned her to death, but the "judges" who wished to apply the penalty imposed by the law lacked the moral authority to condemn her. Jesus, who undoubtedly had such authority, said to her: "Neither do I condemn you" (8:11). The manipulation of the law by those with power is not the way God acts. While before God we are all culpable, not all of us are condemned. It is not surprising that the first Christians had circulated this anecdote widely, in which a woman culpable under the law is not condemned. They understood that the abuse of the law by human beings does not have the approbation of the one who came to reveal God's love, especially when it has to do with the abuse of women.

Neither is it a surprise that *According to John* presents Jesus as "the Resurrection and the Life" (11:25) in dialogues he has with two women: Martha and Mary of Bethany. Even if to start with they reflect the perspective typical of those who do not know who Jesus is or where he comes from, they become guides to the believers. Martha is the one who confesses: "I believe that you are the Christ, the Son of God, he who is coming into the world" (11:27). Mary is the one who pronounces the technical words which are the invitation which this gospel offers to all its readers: "Come and see" (11:34). The invitation to "see" is repeated many times in the gospel. It is offered to human beings who need to see I AM. In the case of Mary, however, with characteristic irony, the invitation is for I AM to see a corpse shrouded in its sepulcher.

It is somewhat confusing that at the beginning of this episode the narrator identifies Mary as the one "who anointed the Lord with ointment and wiped his feet with her hair" (11:2). It is confusing because the narrative of the anointing is found in the next chapter. But just as Nicodemus is known as the one who came to Jesus by night (7:50; 19:39), Mary is the one who "took a pound of costly ointment of pure nard and anointed the feet of Jesus and wiped his feet with her hair" (12:3). Judas (with the hypocrisy of the thief) calculates that the precious liquid was worth three hundred denarii and was being wasted. Jesus, however, interprets Mary's action as the anointing of his body for burial. Actually, this is the real anointing of Jesus' body. The language which describes the details of the anointing carried out by Joseph of Arimathea and Nicodemus tells us that what the gentleman of the night and the secret disciple carried out was a Jewish ritual concerned with the flesh because they did not understand that the Spirit is the one that gives life. The real anointing of the body of Jesus was carried out by a woman who was a true disciple.

In *According to Mark* and *According to Matthew* the anointing is performed by an anonymous woman who has an alabaster jar with a costly ointment of nard and pours it on Jesus' head. To call attention to the action, Jesus prophesies: "Wherever the gospel is preached in the whole world, what she has done will be told in memory of her" (Mk. 14:9; Mt. 26:13). No doubt these words underline the importance of what this woman had done. Her fame is going to be recognized in the whole world, wherever the gospel is preached. No such thing is ever said of one of the twelve disciples. I must confess, however, that the indirect, more poetic, way in which *According to John* underlines the action of Mary of Bethany impresses me more: "the house was filled with the fragrance of her ointment" (12:3). The action of Mary did not have an effect on just Jesus. She gave the whole house a different atmosphere. Jesus does not mention here Mary's future fame wherever the gospel is preached. Her generous identification with the one who was to die had an immediate effect on all those present. The death and resurrection of Lazarus determined Jesus' death and the anointing of his body by Mary represents the deposition of his body. Symbolically, Mary has carried out the burial of the one who died to bear much fruit (12:24).

Mary of Bethany is the one who invites Jesus, saying "Come and see" a four-day-old dead body which already smells bad. She is the one who anoints Jesus' feet to give closure to his death and the one who takes Jesus to the door of the place where he must fulfill the purpose of his incarnation by demonstrating the power of life. Martha confesses to believe in the Resurrection and the Life, and Mary is the one who guides and completes the triumph of Jesus over death. These two women whom Jesus loved (11:5) play a role more important than that of any other disciple in *According to John*.

Magdala is a small village on the western shore of the Sea of Galilee between Tiberias and Capernaum, quite a long way north of Bethany, which is almost a suburb to the East of Jerusalem. Mary of Magdala clearly is not Mary of Bethany, the one who anointed the feet of Jesus. Neither is she the one who guided Jesus to Lazarus' tomb. She is the one who announces the resurrection to the disciples who had closeted themselves "for fear of the Jews" (20:19). What the disciples least expected was to see Jesus again. The possibility of a resurrection had not crossed their minds (20:9). In this story, the empty tomb tells Mary of Magdala that someone has taken the corpse somewhere else. When later Mary realizes that the one speaking to her is not the gardener but Jesus, she runs to give the good news to the disciples: "I have seen the Lord" (20:18). She who had first announced that the body had been stolen, now announces that she has seen and has received instructions from the Lord: "Go to my brethren and say to them, I am ascending to my Father and your Father, to my God and your God" (20:17). In *According to John*, she is the first to see the living Lord after his death on the cross.

Among the first Christians there arose different lists of the first witnesses to the Risen Christ. In 1 Cor. 15:5 – 8, Paul gives two lists. One places Peter first and then the twelve. The other places

James first and then all the apostles. *According to John* places Mary of Magdala first and then the twelve. Apparently different Christian communities traced their origins to the disciple who headed their preferred list. Since she is the one who sees the Living Lord first, it is quite probable that she was among the founding members of the Johannine community. It is quite reasonable to think that she, together with Martha and Mary of Bethany, the Samaritan woman, the mother of Jesus and the beloved disciple, whose identity remains elusive, were among those who formed the nucleus of this community. This select group was the one that "remembered" the meaning of what the disciples had not understood while they traveled the dusty roads of Galilee, Samaria and Judea with Jesus.

Hanging on the cross, Jesus recognizes his mother and the beloved disciple. Instead of negating his earthly family, Jesus constitutes a new family with his mother and the beloved disciple (19:26 – 27). After the resurrection Jesus sends Mary of Magdala to tell "his brethren," the new members of his family, that he is ascending to the Father. There is no doubt that in the Johannine community women enjoyed the prestige of being the ones "who understood all things" and testified to the others. They were the servants of the Comforter, the *Parákletos*. In the same spirit, the gospel *According to Mark* says that while all the male disciples were absent during the crucifixion, the women witnessed everything that took place. Among them was Mary of Magdala, Mary the mother of James the less and Joseph, and Salome. They had been with Jesus in Galilee and had followed and served him there. Also at Golgotha were other women who had come to Jerusalem with Jesus apparently from other places (Mk. 15:40 – 41). This gospel also reports that Mary of Magdala and Mary the mother of Joses witnessed the entombment (Mk. 15:47). *According to John* gives to the women a much more prominent place than that given to them by *According to Mark*. They are not only the faithful "followers" (the technical designation of disciples in *According to Mark*) and are not merely witnesses of the crucifixion and the burial. They are the ones who play the most important roles in the drama of Jesus' mission and the ones who constitute the nucleus of a singularly important Christian community.

18
Clean by the Word

The gospel *According to John* is full of surprises. It might be better to say that it charts a course of its own, and both its novelties and language cause readers to take a second look. Reading this gospel is to sense there is something under the surface that needs to be uncovered. To interpret its peculiarities is not easy, and, as a result, its various interpretations are quite different.

Perhaps this characteristic of the gospel is best displayed in what it says about the sacraments, as they came to be known in the history of Christianity. Sometimes a difference is made between a sacrament and a sacramental act. Thus, baptism and the Lord's Supper are considered sacraments, while the washing of feet is a sacramental act. Sacraments are acts that when performed carry in themselves saving grace. In the mainstream Christian tradition, sacraments can be administered only by an ecclesiastical official while lay people may administer sacramental acts. *According to John* distinguishes itself by not mentioning that Jesus participated in sacraments and by being the only one reporting that Jesus washed the feet of his disciples.

In a previous meditation we noticed that in this gospel it is not said that Jesus was baptized by John the Baptist. *According to John* says that Jesus began his ministry as a baptizer. As such he attracted more people wishing to be baptized than John (3:22; 4:1). This caused the disciples of John to complain that Jesus, who had been endorsed by John's powerful witness, was now competing with him and taking away his public (3:26).

The sacraments were established toward the end of the first century when Christianity was becoming institutionalized and starting to create official channels through which the Holy Spirit could flow under ecclesiastical control. Within this framework, the notion that Jesus had been a baptizer in competition with John became problematic. As a result, an editor of the gospel added the explanation that "Jesus himself did not baptize, but only his disciples" (4:2). From the Johannine perspective it was also problematic that Jesus had been baptized by John. The baptism of John was "of repentance for the forgiveness of sins" (Mk. 1:4). *According to Mark* says that those who came to John to be baptized did it "confessing their sins" (Mk. 1:5). Surely those who considered Jesus to be the incarnate *Logos* could not envision his confessing sins to John. They could, however, think of him as the one who as a baptizer initiated the baptism of water and the Spirit.

According to John makes a clear distinction between the baptism of water administered by John and the baptism administered by Jesus. Jesus' baptism, John the Baptist points out, is "with the Holy Spirit" (1:33). Also to be noticed is that no mention is made of the purpose of John's baptism or of his apocalyptic message (Mt. 3:10). John the Baptist declares: "I came baptizing with water that he might be revealed to Israel (1:31). John's mission is limited to announcing to Israel the coming of the Holy Spirit and the Lamb of God. That is, in this telling his mission has been incorporated into the Johannine theology of the descent of the Son of Man.

It is a bit disconcerting, therefore, to find that most commentators consider this gospel as the New Testament document that provides the basic source for sacramental theology. This judgment is based on interpretations which see the conversation between Jesus and Nicodemus as supporting the sacrament of baptism, and the discourse following the feeding of the five thousand as supporting the sacrament of the Lord's Supper. The texts, however, do not support these interpretations.

The conversation of Jesus with Nicodemus presupposes that Jesus had baptized others and gives the significance of what he had done. Nicodemus does not understand when Jesus says to him: "Unless one is born anew [from above], he cannot see the kingdom of God" (3:3). To make his saying plain, Jesus repeats it with different words: "Unless one is born of water and the Spirit, he cannot enter the kingdom of God" (3:5). To be born from above and to be born of water and the Spirit is one and the same thing. In other words, the baptism of Jesus is not a rite for the remission of sins. It is the creation of a new being by the Spirit.

Here we must pay attention to an aside that seems disconnected from the context. It concerns a dispute about purity between the disciples of John and "the Jews" (3:25). "The Jews" carried out various rites of purification such as lustrations, ritual baths, washing of feet at the court of the temple before approaching the altar, etc. John's baptism was also a rite for the purification from sins. It is not clear which practices were at the center of this dispute. It would appear that the reference to it intends to alert the reader of the difference between the baptism of John and the "baptisms" of "the Jews," and to distinguish the "birth from above" from all rites of purification. While the disciples of John and "the Jews" are involved in a discussion about purifications, Jesus is above it all. His mission is to enable a "birth from above" that triumphs over death, not to introduce means of purification from sin.

That *According to John* devalues purification rites is clear by the way in which the water that Jesus changed into wine is characterized. It was an impressive quantity kept in "stone" containers "for the Jewish rites of purification" (3:6). This attitude is also in evidence in the anointing of the body of Jesus with an extraordinary amount of ointment for its purification according to "the burial custom of the Jews" (19:40). In both cases the purification rituals are ridiculed for the unwarranted attention given to them. We must also note that the narrator says that some days before Passover "many went up … to Jerusalem … to purify themselves" (11:55). Their preoccupation with purity seems to be higher than with the celebration of the liberation from slavery which is at the core of Passover. Also to be noticed is that Jesus' last supper with his disciples was not a Passover supper. Unlike the accounts in the synoptic gospels (Mk. 14:14, 22 – 25), in *According to John* the last supper was neither a Lord's Supper nor a Passover meal. On the following morning, when Jesus was taken before Pilate, the Jews did not enter the praetorium for fear of defiling themselves and thereby being unable to eat the Passover meal that night (18:28). Throughout the gospel purification rituals are devalued.

In the discourse of chapter six, Jesus declares himself to be the bread of life that came down from heaven. This bread is superior to the manna that fell from the sky as a response to Moses' mediation during the Exodus (6:48 – 49). Jesus had already promised that "he who comes to me shall never hunger, and he who believes in me shall never thirst" (6:35). Those who ate manna in the desert, of course, soon became hungry again. This promise is repeated with different words: "If any one eats of this bread, he will live for ever; and the bread which I shall give for the life of the world is my flesh" (6:51). The theme reaches its climax with the following explanation: "He who eats my flesh and drinks my blood abides in me and I in him … he who eats me will live because of me" (6:56 – 57). Thus the contrasts between manna and the Son who descended from heaven are clearly drawn: one came down from the sky while the other came down from heaven, one provided energy for a few more hours of life in the flesh while the other provides eternal life in the Spirit, the one is to be eaten with the mouth while the other is to be eaten with the heart.

The elaboration of the notion that Jesus is the bread from heaven is noteworthy for the way in which the verbs follow a predictable sequence. It begins with "he who comes" and "he who believes," then identifies "he who eats" and culminates with "he who abides." To come, to see, to believe, to eat and to abide are, as we shall see in another meditation, technical terms in the Johannine vocabulary. Here we do not have an explanation of a ritual with material symbols. Here the concern is with a life that *abides* in the reality of the birth from water and the Spirit. Failing to understand what Jesus has said, the disciples complain, "This is a hard saying; who can listen to it?" (6:60). Jesus then gives the whole discourse its proper context: "It is the Spirit that gives life, the flesh is of no avail; the words that I have spoken to you are Spirit and life" (6:63). These words echo what Jesus had said to Nicodemus when he did not understand: "That which is born of the flesh is flesh, and that which is born of the Spirit is spirit" (3:6). These declarations aim to deny the efficacy of material objects to stand for the reality of the Spirit.

Both declarations deny value to the flesh. It is not effective even as a symbol or agent of life, that is, as a sacrament. To come, to see, to believe, to eat and to abide can only be done in the realm of the Spirit, where the words of him who is The Word (*Logos*) work as agents of eternal life. It is only in the Spirit that those who believe abide in Jesus and Jesus in them. Neither the birth from above nor the bread that descended from heaven and abides without spoiling from one day to the next are repeatable events; they are endowments that constitute a life that abides without fleshly supports.

According to John says that Jesus had a last supper with his disciples (13:1), and that during it he washed the feet of his disciples and identified Judas as the one who would betray him. This supper, however, did not include the institution of the bread and the wine as symbols of his blood and flesh. In other words, the last supper was not a Lord's Supper. The account of the supper, in fact, says nothing about the supper, in that it is like the narrative of the wedding feast at Cana which tells nothing about the actual wedding. It is concerned with things that happened during it. These events are introduced with a complicated periodic sentence:

> Before the feast of Passover,
> Jesus knowing that his hour had come
> for him to go up from this world to the Father,
> loving his own who were in the world he loved them to the end,
> and while supper was going on
> knowing that the Father had given all things into his hands

and that he had come from God and was going to God,
He raises himself from supper and placing his garments aside
and taking a piece of coarse cloth he girded himself. (13:1 – 2, 4, my translation)

This tells us that Jesus' hour to return to the Father had come, and he dressed for the trip. With typical irony, the one who is acknowledged by all to be Teacher and Lord (13:13) dresses himself as servant. It is a radical demonstration that his "hour" does not only involve his "glorification" (12:23); it also calls for his servitude. After having performed the washing of the feet, which should have taken place before supper, at the arrival of the guests, Jesus explains the didactic function of what he has done: "If I then, your Lord and Teacher, have washed your feet, you also ought to wash one another's feet. For I have given you an example, that you also should do as I have done to you" (13:14 – 15).

The meaning of the action is given in the dialogue between Jesus and Peter. When Peter declares: "You shall never wash my feet," Jesus makes the washing of the feet indispensable: "If I do not wash you, you have no part in me" (13:8). It turns out, then, that without the washing of the feet, as without the birth from above, it is impossible to enter into the kingdom and have a part in Jesus. The reason is that this washing leaves the one who receives it clean: "He who is washed … is clean all over" (13:10).

That select group of disciples received the washing of their feet by the hands of Jesus, but since then Christians normally do not receive the washing of their feet by an ecclesiastical official. After washing their feet Jesus explained that what he had done was to give an example. Then he gave them a command: "… you also ought to wash one another's feet" (13:14). To give his example even more significance, Jesus added a beatitude: "If you know these things, blessed are you if you do them" (13:17). This beatitude is anchored on a conditional sentence which tells us that doing is more important than knowing.

In *According to John* Jesus is not baptized, does not celebrate a Lord's Supper, and does not institute bread and wine as sacraments that need to be administered by authorized clergy. Jesus only institutes the washing of the feet which must be administered by everyone to everyone, in this way democratizing the kingdom of heaven.

Jesus refers to himself as one who was consecrated (or sanctified) and sent by the Father (10:36), and he also asks the Father to sanctify, or consecrate, his disciples (17:17). These references to the consecration of the one sent by the Father and the ones being sent by him do not imply their ordination to a sacred, priestly office that authorizes those consecrated to perform sacred rituals. As the farewell prayer of Jesus clearly states, their sanctification does not set them apart for ritual leadership. They are set apart, sanctified, by the truth: "Sanctify them in the truth; thy word is truth" (17:17). Their participation in the truth, the way and the life that Jesus came to reveal is what sets all his disciples apart, both theologically and socially. Their sanctification does not establish a hierarchy within the community.

As an explanation of his washing of the disciples' feet Jesus said: "Truly, truly, I say to you, a servant is not greater than his master; nor is he who is sent [an apostle] greater than he who sent him" (13:16). It is somewhat baffling that the commandment to enact the example given by Jesus is justified by a declaration which, though introduced with the rhetorical force of "Truly, truly I say to you," is, after all, quite banal. Who does not know that the servant is not greater than his master? The more specific repetition of the idea, however, seems to reveal its import. For this Christian community it is important to emphasize that the apostle is not greater than the one sending him. No doubt these words are aimed at the apostles who took themselves too seriously and had illusions of grandeur. Paul also had to deal with such "super apostles" (2 Cor. 11:5). Toward the end of the first century, when the Christian movement was turning into an ecclesiastical institution, and divine grace was beginning to be "controlled" by clergy authorized to administer sacraments, the Johannine community insisted that "it is not by measure that God gives the Spirit" (3:34). The Spirit cannot be administered in small doses or found in the routine of rituals. Like the wind, it blows from where it wishes to sustain the life of those born by its power.

Jesus ended his discourse about eating the bread that descended from heaven by declaring that the flesh is of no avail, but "the words that I have spoken to you are Spirit and life" (6:63). Later he said: "If any one keeps my word, he will never see death" (8:51). In the same manner, most likely in reference to the washing of the feet that makes the whole person clean, Jesus tells the disciples: "You are already made clean by the word which I have spoken to you ... If you abide in me, and my words abide in you, ask whatever you will, and it shall be done for you" (15:3, 7).

If as servants they wash each other's feet, making them clean, they abide in him, and his words abide in them. Then Jesus no longer considers them servants. They consider him Teacher and Lord, and he considers them now his "friends, for all I have heard from my Father I have made known to you" (15:15). In this way those who wash each other's feet are identified with the one who has returned to his God and our God. The cleansing carried out by the words that Jesus has spoken allows humans to come, to see, to believe, to eat and to abide as friends who know what their Teacher and Lord does. As Peter would understand later, now we also can understand. No rite of purification, argues *According to John*, can produce the mutual abiding that the Word can produce. The Johannine community is a sisterhood and brotherhood (20:17) of "friends" (15:15) of Jesus who abide in him without the aid of material props. It is a lay community that rejects the institutionalization of their spiritual life and any attempts to control the Holy Spirit by ecclesiastical authority. The Christian life consists of abiding in his word (8:31), and confessing, as did Peter, "You have the words of eternal life" (6:68).

19

WE MUST WORK WHILE IT IS DAY

According to John reports three healing miracles: that of the son of the imperial official (4:46 – 54), that of the sick man at the pool of Bethesda (5:1 – 16) and that of the man born blind (9:1 – 14). In two of these narratives, after the details of the miracle have been described, it is said that the healing took place on a Sabbath. These healings included actions which the rabbinic interpretation of the fourth commandment prohibited on a Sabbath. Jesus instructed the sick man to carry his bed home, and he himself made mud by mixing dust and spittle. The other healing, it is specifically explained, took place at the seventh hour of a non-specified day.

After the Babylonian Exile the synagogue became an important new institution. Its place in Judaism, however, was not meant to be in any way a substitute for the temple that had been rebuilt in Jerusalem and was declared the only place in the whole world where sacrifices to Yahve could be offered. Synagogues were primarily places that promoted the study of the Torah and served as community centers. In them, the Scribes became the ones who determined the proper way to apply the injunctions of the law to daily life. Among the commandments, the one requiring cessation from work on Sabbaths became the object of much debate. On Sabbaths life went on. What could and could not be done needed to be determined. To better regulate its observance, the rabbis searched for a way to define what is *work*. Their search took them to the instructions given by God for the building of the sanctuary (Ex.

35:4 – 39:43), where thirty nine different tasks are identified. The rabbis decided that this list of labors required for the construction of the tabernacle defines that which is not permitted to be done on the Sabbath. To carry a burden and to prepare a mixture are both on the list.

Both Sabbath healings in *According to John* unleash arguments to defend Jesus' authority to establish what is permitted and what is not permitted to be done on a Sabbath. Such questions came up frequently among Jews, and no doubt were also asked by Christians. All of them, at the beginning, were Jews, and ceasing to be Jews did not even enter their minds. In the first century of our era, the Sabbath was one of the most important identity marks among Jews, and its observance was one of the few things that Gentiles knew about them. In other words, early Christians did not ask themselves whether as followers of Christ they should continue to observe the Sabbath; that was taken for granted. The question was, "What is being forbidden by the Sabbath commandment?" The list of the thirty nine works the rabbis had extracted from Ex. 35:4 – 39:43 did not include many of the activities that had become common in Hellenistic urban centers. Thus, the question had much relevance. Are the thirty nine activities listed to be understood as self-referentially limiting, or are they to be interpreted as the headings of categories that involve many other similar *works*? The difference between Jews in general and those who proclaimed the Risen Christ was that the Jews solved this problem by citing a passage of Scripture. Christians, besides citing Scripture, would also appeal to the Sabbath conduct of Jesus as a clue to a solution.

The healing of the sick man at the pool of Bethesda is given two justifications, and I will consider them separately. Surely 7:19 – 23 refers to the healing of this sick man. In these verses we find an argument *a fortiori*, from minor to major. If one admits that in one case a certain rule applies, *how much more* must be admitted that in this other case another rule applies. The argument works if common sense, or an official determination, considers that this other case is more important than the first one.

In the case of the sick man at the pool, the argument is based on what the Jews had decided on circumcision when the eighth day of birth fell on a Sabbath. To carry out the circumcision requires doing things found in the list of the thirty nine works prohibited on a Sabbath. This created a true dilemma. What must be done when obeying one law of the Scriptures involves breaking another law of the Scriptures? In this case the Jews had determined that the law of circumcision was to be given preference over the law of the Sabbath. Circumcision is the mark of the true Jew. The Sabbath, according to rabbinic thought, is to be kept only by Jews. The rabbis spoke of the Sabbath as a Jew's bride with whom he is indelibly bound. Gentiles cannot share the bridal chamber reserved for Jews only. It was, therefore, most important to circumcise Jews first so that they might legitimately keep the Sabbath.

While circumcision was the mark of the members of the chosen people of God, with time it also came to be considered something that perfected, that added qualities to the male body. This is the basis for the argument of 7:19 – 23. If you consider it licit to perfect a member of the body by removing the foreskin on a Sabbath, how much more should you consider it licit to give health to a whole body on a Sabbath. Common sense says that the whole body is more important than one of its members.

We find this type of argument also, for example, in the defense of the disciples who harvested wheat and ate it on a Sabbath (Mk. 2:23 – 28). If you consider it to be licit for David and his men to eat the sanctuary's bread of the presence, how much more should you consider it licit for my disciples to eat wheat harvested on a Sabbath because my presence with my disciples is superior to the presence of David with his men. Of course, this argument works only among those who admit the superiority of Christ over David. This tells us that the early Christians held different opinions as to what is licit Sabbath activity, and that they appealed to the conduct of Jesus in order to determine permissible Sabbath activity. It also lets us see that the early Christians were well educated in Greek culture. They could develop logical arguments as the most effective way to arrive at wise conclusions. These kinds of arguments were not part of traditional Hebrew culture as preserved in the Wisdom Literature. In that tradition, parallelisms based on free association of ideas are the standard method for expanding the intellectual horizon and drawing conclusions.

Besides the argument based on the priority of circumcision, the healing of the sick man at the pool of Bethesda is also justified in verse 17 of chapter 5: "My Father works until now, and I work" (my translation). This justification of Jesus' Sabbath conduct is based on the answer to a question that preoccupied the ancient Jews: "Does God keep God's laws?" More specifically, "Does God keep the Sabbath?" This question does not come up in our day because we understand that nature functions by itself according to what are commonly called "natural laws." This way of seeing nature is relatively recent. When Isaac Newton proposed that the earth and all the stars in the heavens follow their respective orbits controlled by the law of gravity, many Christians thought he was negating the existence of God. They thought that God is the one who has in his hands the movements of the heavenly bodies. The rising and the setting of the sun take place because God causes the sun to come up at dawn and to go down at dusk. If God keeps the Sabbath, ceasing to work and resting, the sun would not come up, and many other things would not occur. Since every Sabbath the sun comes up at dawn and nature keeps functioning normally it can only mean that God works on the Sabbath.

In the writings of the Rabbis and of Philo of Alexandria different explications are given for the fact that God works on Sabbaths. For example, it is adduced that God works on material things during the other days of the week, but on Sabbaths God works on spiritual and intellectual matters. Among other things, Philo explains that God is at perfect rest also while working. In other words, it was argued that it was possible for God to work and at the same time keep the Sabbath commandment that ordered abstention from work.

When Jesus says, "My Father works until now," he is saying that God works continuously, including Sabbaths. It is not true that God worked only in a remote past to bring about creation and has been at rest ever since. NO! God works every day. The Jews who heard this affirmation were in complete agreement with it. Jesus, however, added, "and I work" every day, also. Here he was not making an *a fortiori* argument, from minor to major. This is an ontological argument; it appeals to the nature of his being. Jesus claims to have, like God, the prerogative to work on Sabbaths. The Jews had no difficulty understanding what he had said. The narrator reports: "And this was why the Jews sought all the more to kill him, because he not only broke the Sabbath but also called God his Father, making himself equal with God" (5:18). Jesus' claim was a direct challenge to the one fundamental doctrine of the Jews after the Babylonian Exile: God is One.

These few words to justify the healing of the sick man at the pool give to the narrative a twist and provide the opportunity to elaborate on the Sabbath activities of the Son. In verses 19 – 30 the work that the Son carries out on a daily basis, inclusive of Sabbaths, is to give life and to judge. These are also exclusive divine prerogatives. That is, the Son is not only equal to God, his Father, but is also able to do what only God can do. Jesus had healed the sick man and ordered him to carry his bed home. He had given life to the sick and had judged those who in ignorance judged him.

The declaration "My Father works until now," however, leaves us a bit confused because of its temporal reference. To which "now" does it refer? This question has kept scholars busy for some time. Is it the case that God ceased working when Jesus died on the cross? Is not the activity of the Comforter, the Spirit of Truth, a continuation of the work of the Son, which also is carried on every day? Or, is not the Sabbath work of the Son being performed now by his disciples? These questions, actually, are reducible to one: "What is the eschatological meaning of 'until now'?"

Undoubtedly the phrase has a temporal reference, but it is not clear when "until now" comes to an end. The one thing we can tell is that "now" is when the work of the Son is synchronized to the work of the Father, and, as the discourse that follows in verses 19 – 47 show, "now" is a critical moment when the presence of the Son on earth obliges human beings to make a decision about his person. This decision makes the difference between life and death. The gospel *According to John*, as we noted in a previous meditation, considers the presence of the giver of eternal life "now" as the fulfillment of all that "Moses in the law and the prophets wrote" (1:45). The "now" of God the Father and God the Son is humanity's eschatological moment. It is when what is ultimately vital imposes itself requiring a decision. In other words, the "until now" says much about what is going on, but says nothing about the future. It makes the present the culmination of a process.

The justification for the healing of the sick man at the pool is linked to the words of Jesus before healing the man born blind: "We must work the works of him who sent me while it is day; night comes when no one can work" (9:4). It is during the day, "now," while the Light of the world is here, that the works the Father wishes to be done must be accomplished. That is, the Sabbath is not like the night when no one can work, but like the day, when the work of judging and giving life must be done. As long as the Son is on earth it is day; it is Sabbath. He is the Light of the World (9:15), and the sons of light (12:36), those who have been born of God (1:13), work "now" even on the Sabbath.

According to John has a well developed concept of time. In previous meditations we saw how incidents in the life of Jesus are framed by Jewish feasts that provide the context for their interpretation. We also noted the way in which "the third day" and "the hour," with special attention to "the hour that *now* is," are used theologically. Besides, while Jesus and his disciples are beings of the day, Judas (13:30) and Nicodemus (3:2; 7:50; 19:39) are creatures of the night. The revelation of Jesus in glory as the Savior of the World takes place at high noon, when the sun is at its zenith (4:6, 19:14). On this point this gospel disagrees with the apocalyptic expectations that envision the eschatological drama culminating at midnight; the Lord will come when least expected, like a thief in the night. In the synoptic gospels Jesus died at three o'clock in the afternoon, the ninth hour [Mk. 15:34], rather than at high noon. In *According to John* time is at the service of theology, and the Sabbath has become the day in which the work of God must be done, that is, at all times.

It is no coincidence that the third healing narrated in *According to John* also makes a specific reference to time. Even though Jesus is not in the presence of the child about to die, at the moment when Jesus, being in Cana of Galilee, says to the officer, "Your son will live," in that very moment the child in Capernaum ceased having a fever. This took place on the seventh hour, the one with the perfect number (4:52). The significance of this is that the words of Jesus to the imperial official had their fulfillment "now," and in this case the "now" is at the seventh hour. Besides, the absent Jesus also brings healing to the Gentiles "now." It is during the day when the Son is among women and men "now," that eternal life, or its opposite, is received by human beings. It is "now" that the ultimate purpose of the Sabbath as the celebration of freedom and life is being accomplished.

Some among the Jews and among the early Christians conceived life with God temporally as an eternal Sabbath. *According to John* distinguishes itself by emphasizing that God works "until now," "while it is day." "Now" is when Christians who possess eternal life (3:15, 16, 36; 5:24; 6:40, 47, 54; 20:31) must do even greater works than those done by the Son (14:12). That which the Son does, Christians must also do. As the Father and the Son, they work on Sabbath. In other words, they live in a perennial Sabbath. Like God, they can also enjoy the Sabbath rest while doing the works of God every day of their lives. The Glorified Christ established the eschatological Sabbath in which the "children of the Light" work to bring more life to the world because they must work while it is day.

20

UNITED BY LOVE

"You shall love the Lord your God with all your heart, and with all your soul, and with all your might" (Deut. 6:5). This commandment seems out of place in our day. Is it possible to love under duress? For us, love must be spontaneous, must come out from the inside. It is impossible to be obligated to love. We understand love to be basically a feeling of the soul that is difficult to explain. As Pascal said, love has its reasons which are not to be reasoned with. To order another to love is to provoke a negative reaction. It is to devalue his personality by taking away the innermost aspect of his being. We understand love in the romantic tradition that sees all beings related to each other in nature and thinks that love is the force that unites individuals who know that they belong to a primordial unity. Romanticism considers human beings as integral members of the natural order. Romantic love has its roots in the subjective and unmediated depths of our being that, rising to the surface, express themselves passionately even when controlled by social mores.

In the Old Testament, however, love is choosing, preferring. That is, it is an exercise of the will. The vocabulary of classical Hebrew has neither words that describe mental states or capacities nor words with which to study our subjective activities the way we do today. It does not have the words "mind," "reason," "will," "argument," "conscience," etc. Mental and psychological functions are located in parts of the body. The heart is the organ of the will, not of feelings and emotions. These are found in the stomach and the intestines, the entrails. It makes sense, therefore, to command others to love with all their heart, that is, with singleness of purpose.

This way of expressing the idea is also found, for example, in the beatitude of the pure in heart, or of a simple heart (Mt. 5:8). Those incapable of deciding what they want have two hearts, rather than a well integrated, single, pure heart.

If to love is to choose, to prefer, the commandment to love God with all your heart is perfectly understandable. To love God is to choose God with singleness of will, rather than other gods. The perennial temptation of the Israelites was to serve the gods of the Canaanites. To love and serve Yahve is said to have been the requisite that Moses put before the people prior to entering the land of Canaan. On the other hand, Israel is the chosen people loved by Yahve. Even though Amos and Isaiah recognized that Yahve was also involved with the history of other nations, for them, undoubtedly, Israel was the chosen people with whom Yahve had made a covenant. Israel is the apple of God's eye. It is the chosen, preferred, loved people of God. It was, therefore, not unreasonable to order the people to love God in return. That is, to make God their preferred choice.

Here, neither hate nor love implies the powerful visceral sentiments that we connect to them today. In particular, hate does not have the connotations of powerful sentiments of enmity or dislike provoked by prejudices or desires for vengeance. Modern romantic notions that dramatize these states of mind should not be read back into ancient documents. That Isaac loved Esau, but Rebecca loved Jacob (Gen. 25:28) only tells us which son was preferred by each of the parents. That Jacob loved Rachel (Gen. 29:18), but Leah was hated (Gen. 29:31), tells us that Jacob loved Rachel more than Leah (Gen 29:30). That is, Leah was not his preferred wife. This usage also appears in Jesus' declaration: "He who loves his life loses it, and he who hates his life in this world will keep it for eternal life" (12:25). Jesus also makes the point that those who hate him hate his Father also (15:23 – 24); that is, they prefer someone else. The narrator explains that this fulfills what is written in "their law," but is actually said by the psalmist (Ps. 35:19; 69:4). In these texts to love and to hate contrast the uses of the will and the need to make a choice. Today any one who hates his life in this world is diagnosed as mentally ill. The point being made, however, is against making life in "this world" the preferred choice.

According to John, as noted in a previous meditation, maybe more than any other New Testament document, breathes the atmosphere of the Old Testament. Even though a dualism between the flesh and the Spirit is pervasive in it, and it utilizes the Greek vocabulary with evident nuance and a broad understanding of its philosophical connotations, it presupposes good knowledge of the Jewish traditions. This cultural richness is evident in the way it presents Jesus' new commandment: "A new commandment I give to you, that you love one another; even as I have loved you, that you also love one another" (13:34, cp. 15:17). Like the commandment that they should wash each other's feet, this new commandment is addressed to the community of disciples. Its fulfillment will be their identity card as a community. "By this all men will know that you are my disciples, if you have love for one another" (13:35). It will also be their strength.

That to love continues to be understood as to choose or to prefer is evident in the references to the "beloved disciple," that is the preferred one. The message that Lazarus is sick comes to Jesus as, "Lord, he whom you love is ill" (11:3). This distinction is then relativized by the explanation: "Now Jesus loved Martha and her sister and Lazarus" (11:5), that is, all three were preferred friends. Something quite different is going on when the narrator says that on his way to Lazarus' tomb Jesus wept, and "the Jews" interpreted this saying: "See how he loved him!" (11:35-36). This scene is another one of those full of irony in which things are not what they appear. The interpretation of "the Jews" is undoubtedly evidence of their lack of understanding. Jesus had not come to Bethany to console those in mourning, or to become a mourner himself. Of course, Jesus loved Lazarus, but he had come to Bethany so that "the Son of God may be glorified" (11:4). To think that Jesus wept because a close friend had died is to deny that he is the resurrection and the life.

In the farewell discourses Jesus refers to the mutual love of the Father and the Son. This love manifests the glory that the Father has given to the Son because he has loved him since "before the foundation of the world" (17:24). This glory is veiled during the Son's pilgrimage on earth. The Son's crucifixion, which in reality is his "lifting up" and his return to the Father, is declared to be his "glorification." It is so because the unity of the Father and the Son founded in their mutual love is restored when the Son is lifted up to the region "above"— that is, when he returns to the place whence he came. The Son is glorified when he reveals to all humanity the unity that love established.

What Jesus desires, about which he insists in the farewell discourses, is that the glory of the love that establishes unity be a reality in the community of his disciples. He wishes that this glory be the glory of his disciples also (17:22). The love that projects the glory of God is not the romantic love that is based on the subjectivity that all creatures share in nature. It is the love that unites the Father and the Son who share the divine Being. As a consequence, as Jesus says, the Son only does the will of the Father (14:31); he "abides" in the love of the Father (15:10). The union accomplished by this love projects glory. The glue that produces a union without glory cannot be the love that constitutes the unity in the divine Being. Of course, the unity of the divine Being is not a sentimental attachment, but the unity produced by the pure love of a unified will.

According to John gives us a definition of love that is not quite the act of preferring or choosing, characteristic of Hebrew thought; nor is it the emotional attachment of the Greeks which is based on natural, internal impulses, even when conceived less subjectively profound than it was by the nineteenth century Romantics. In this gospel love is more than the preference expressed by choosing or a subjective force that wishes to possess the other. Johannine love is the agent of unity in the divine Being. *According to John* gives us not only a new definition of love as the foundation and the agent of unity; it also gives us a new definition of the glory of God. Rather than being an emanation of power, glory is the manifestation of the love that accomplishes the full union of those who remain who they are. The Father is not the Son, and the Son is not the Father. The two, however, are one because they are united by true love in their singleness of purpose.

Probably, the biblical verse most often recited is the one that says: "For God so loved the world that he gave his only Son, that whoever believes in him should not perish but have eternal life" (3:16). Normally it is assumed that those who love wish to incorporate another unto themselves or to enlarge their own consciousness and participate in another's suffering. The first thing that catches our attention in these words is that God demonstrates his love for the world by giving, relinquishing the Son. But God does not give him indiscriminately. God gives him for a well defined purpose. God gives him to enlarge the circle of those who are united. God gives the Son so that once lifted up, glorified, he could become the object of faith that must be seen by all human beings (3:15). God gives him so that those who see him lifted up, those who believe in him should have eternal life participating in his life. In this gospel, both *to believe* and *to love* appear almost exclusively as verbs or participles. Those who hear and believe are those who love. Faith is not the ability to agree with a doctrinal proposition. *Faith*, like *love*, is a power that unites and gives life. The glorification of the Son, which reveals the unity of the Father and the Son in mutual love, is the agent of love that unites the *believers* in a community that reveals the glory of God and attracts others to God's love.

As the good shepherd who lays down his life for his sheep, Jesus calls his sheep from the cross (10:6), and his sheep, who know his voice, follow him. As the flock that follows him they are united by their trust in the shepherd. As the Son knows the Father and the Father knows the Son, so also the sheep know the voice of their shepherd. Eventually even the sheep which are "not of this fold" will also hear the voice of the good shepherd … "so there shall be one flock, one shepherd" (10:15 – 16). The power of the love that unites the Father and the Son and causes the Father to give the Son to the "world" is to be the power that unifies the Christian community that testifies to the glory of God. Jesus' willingness to lay down his life, which is the reason why the Father loves him (10:17), is also the power that unites all Christians in one fold.

It is no coincidence that the narrator's interpretation of the High Priest's reasoning for putting Jesus to death — it is better that one man die than for the nation to be destroyed (11:50 – 52) — is followed by the account of the anointing of Jesus by Mary, the sister of Martha and Lazarus. The event took place six days before Passover at a supper in which "Martha served, and Lazarus was sitting at the table with him" (12:1 - 2). Jesus establishes the significance of Mary's action in his rebuke of Judas, who thought that three hundred denarii were being wasted. Jesus says: "Let her alone, let her keep it for the day of my burial" (12:7). Many students of this gospel have pointed out that in it the raising of Lazarus is tied to Jesus' death, and the anointing of Mary enacts his burial. As said in a previous meditation, the account of the anointing and burial performed by a "secret" disciple and a gentleman of "the night" is a sarcastic demonstration of what can be expected of those who do not understand who Jesus really is. They are concerned with a dead body of flesh and the customs of "the Jews" (19:38 – 41).

By Jesus' time the Jews had already classified good works as works of justice and works of mercy. The giving of alms, for example, was considered a work of justice. It is an attempt to minimize economic inequality. The anointing of a body for burial, on the other hand, was considered a work of mercy. It actualizes participation in the human condition. The basic difference between works of justice and works of mercy is that the latter require the doers to see themselves in the one benefiting from their action. Those who anoint a body for burial cannot fail to recognize their own mortality as they identify themselves with the one whose body they are preparing for burial.

Mary's anointing of Jesus was a dramatic demonstration of the love that spends itself when one person identifies with another. Her anointing of the feet of Jesus parallels Jesus' washing of the disciples' feet. Anointing the feet was sufficient to make the whole body clean. Unlike Joseph of Arimathea and Nicodemus, who brought one hundred pounds of myrrh and aloes to the tomb, Mary brought one pound of pure nard (12:3) to show the love that united her to her Lord. The quantity was sufficient, the value was extraordinary, and "the house was filled with the fragrance of the ointment." In other words, her action had immense consequences.

In the Lukan version of the story of the anointing, which does not take place in Passion Week, we learn that an unidentified woman known by the host as a sinner washed Jesus' feet with her tears, kissed them and, like Mary, dried the feet with her hair (Lk. 7:37 – 39). In this version the action of the woman is interpreted by Jesus by the parable of the two debtors. Given the great difference between the amounts of debt that were pardoned, Jesus asks: "Now which of them will love him more?" In this version the love of the woman is at center stage and is given a strong emotional touch by the fact that the washing is with tears and is accompanied by kisses. In both versions the anointing is done on the feet and the drying is with her hair. The Markan (Mk. 14:3 – 9) and the Matthean (Mt. 26:6 -13) accounts of the incident have the woman pouring the ointment on Jesus' head, thus giving to the action royal, messianic connotations.

In *According to John* the story lacks the emotional impact of tears and kisses and the royal connotation of an anointing of the head. It focuses on the burial aspects of the anointing and the woman's freedom to spend her money in an act of loving identification with the one already condemned to death. She had already been identified as belonging to a trio loved by Jesus (11:5) and now is shown united in loving devotion to the one who is to be buried. As such, the story is the perfect exemplification of the love that unites the believer with the object of faith. This is the meaning of love: it makes one of the believer and the one who was given by God to save the world. As an act of mercy, anointing is considered the most patent demonstration of love as the power that makes two into one. While the Lukan version of the story makes love the proper response to forgiveness, a Lukan main motif, the Johannine version concentrates on the very costly pure nard that demonstrates the total identification of Mary with Jesus in a central act of mercy. In *According to Luke* love is given strong emotional overtones with tears and kisses. In *According to John* love is the power that unites Mary to Jesus in a heuristic act of mercy. This act of Mary is echoed when Jesus washes the feet of his disciples and commands them to wash each other's feet in imitation of their Lord and Master, thus expanding it to a communal setting (13:14 – 15). As argued in a previous meditation, the washing of the feet in the Johannine community seems to have been understood as an act of identification in surrender to death under persecution. The humble washing of the feet with water or their anointing with pure nard are acts of mercy that unite those who remain themselves. In this way the divine love that makes the Father and the Son to be one is fully present in the earthly life of communities of believers.

The Christian community that is united by love rather than by power, knowledge or authority reveals both the love and the glory of God. In such a community the commandments of Jesus, not the law of Moses that Jesus describes as "your law," are the ones taken to heart. "He who has *my* commandments and keeps them, he it is who loves me; and he who loves me will be loved by my Father, and I will love him and manifest myself to him" (14:21). The fulfillment of the commandments of Jesus is tied to the love of the Father and the Son and causes the Son to manifest himself in those who keep them. The commandment of Jesus is that his disciples love one another. This will cause him to manifest himself in them, and the world will recognize them as his disciples.

The first *Letter of John*, a document that reflects circumstances some years later in the history of the Johannine community, gives the final definition to this way of seeing things: "God is love" (1 Jn. 4:8). Those who are born of God (1:13; 1 Jn. 4:7) hear the voice of their shepherd and follow him (10:4). They are the manifestation of the love that produces unity in the Father and the Son and in the community of the disciples. The Christian community that is united manifests the glory of the Father and the Son (17:26). The love that unites it is founded in the ultimate reality of the divine Being: "That they may all be one; even as thou, Father, art in me, and I in thee, that they also may be in us, so that the world may believe that thou hast sent me" (17:21).

Jesus' essential doctrine was an open challenge to the only fundamental doctrine of the Jews: that God is One. When "the Jews" detect that Jesus claims to have the prerogatives that only God has, and thus was "making himself equal with God," they intensify their desire to kill him (5:18). When Jesus declares: "I and the Father are one," they take up stones again to kill him (10:30 – 31). When Jesus qualifies this declaration saying: "the Father is in me and I am in the Father," they again try to arrest him (10:38 – 39). These declarations were made in public, and they sparked accusations of blasphemy: "…you, being a man, make yourself God" (10:33). When he was alone with his disciples Jesus emphasized that his oneness with the Father is founded on love. On this basis he presented an alternative to the definition that God is one, so dear to "the Jews": The Father, the Son and all his disciples are One. Analyzing the words of Caiaphas, the narrator explains that what the high priest of that year said was, in reality, a prophecy of the significance of the crucifixion: "Jesus should die for the nation, and not for the nation only, but to gather into one the children of God who are scattered abroad" (11:51 – 52). The love that unites the Father and the Son "gathers into one" all those born of God (1:13) who are still dispersed throughout the world.

The "world" will believe in the Son as the One Sent by the Father only when it sees the Christian community united by love and keeping the commandment to love each other (17:21, 23). This will give the glory that has its origin in the unity of the Father and the Son to the community that believes and loves: "The glory which thou hast given me I have given to them, that they may be one even as we are one" (17:22). In such community Jesus does not only manifest himself (14:21). He is actually "in them" (17:26). The glorified Christ is not absent. He abides in the midst of those who abide in the love of the Father and the Son: "If anyone loves me, he will keep my word, and my Father will love him, and we will come to him and make our home [abode] with him" (14:23). God does not abide in temples (4:21), but in those who love God and identify themselves with their incarnated Lord as loving servants who perform acts of mercy. For this reason Jesus advises his disciples: "Abide in my love" (15:9). Those who do this have become one with the Father and the Son.

21

JESUS WEPT

That Jesus wept has been understood to demonstrate the humanity of Jesus better than any other piece of evidence. His ability to read people's minds, perform miracles, exorcise demons, alter the physical qualities of things to enable him to walk on water and change water into wine, is seen as evidence of his divinity, or at least of his special connection with God. For him to need a break in a quiet place, to tire from a long journey on foot, to need to drink and eat, to have strong emotional reactions to what is going on around him, to break down and weep demonstrates Jesus' humanity, his special connection with all mortal human beings.

In *According to John* we learn that Jesus asked the Samaritan woman for a drink, but apparently, if she gave it to him, he did not actually drink it. After the disciples came back from buying food at the nearby town of Sychar, he did not eat it. On the other hand, this gospel reports the most dramatic miracles: changing water into wine, walking on water, and taking a ship out of the middle of a stormy sea and placing it on the shore to which the disciples were going. It also reports the miraculous catch of 153 large fishes, the dream catch of every fisherman before commercial fishing factories began to plow the oceans.

The synoptic gospels report that Jesus brought to life people who had died, but had not yet been buried. *According to John* reports the raising of a man who had been buried for four days. The body had begun the process of decomposition and exuded a bad odor. The telling of this miracle is not just a quick, almost passing reference, as is the case with the raising of the son of the widow of Nain (Lk. 7:11 – 16) or with the raising of the daughter of Jairus

(Mk. 5:22 – 23, 35 – 43; Lk. 8:41 – 42, 49 – 56). The raising of Lazarus plays a crucial role in the drama of Jesus' life in *According to John*. While in the synoptics the cleansing of the temple causes the decision of "the Jews" to put Jesus to death, in this gospel the raising of Lazarus is given credit for it. News of the raising of Lazarus spread like wild fire among the people who became eager to see the beneficiary of this miracle. This caused "the Jews" to become frustrated by their inability to control the new popularity enjoyed by Jesus. Their frustration made them decide to put Lazarus also to death (12:10).

The account of Lazarus' illness, death and resurrection is told with great narrative skills as more and more circumstantial details surrounding it build to a climax. Thus the story not only plays a crucial role in the drama of Jesus' life, but also serves to fully display the theology of the gospel. To get its message one must be aware that the ironic tone that pervades the whole gospel is in full display here.

The story begins with Jesus and his disciples on the other side of the Jordan. They had gone there to get away from "the Jews" who were intent on stoning Jesus for what they considered to be his blasphemous claims. We are not told how long they had been there, more or less in hiding, when Mary and Martha, the sisters of Lazarus, sent word from Bethany that "he whom you love is ill" (11:3). Then we are told that, actually, Jesus "loved Martha and her sister and Lazarus," all three of them. The implicit call for help from those he loved, no doubt, should have elicited a quick response on the part of Jesus. Hearing the news, however, he stayed where he was for two more days. It would appear that Jesus thought that his safety was more important than the well being of those he loved. That he remained in Transjordan for two additional days may have had special significance to those writing this gospel. We also read that he stayed two days with the Samaritans who took him into the town of Sychar (4:40). Is this a coincidence or a significant detail? I can only wonder.

At the end of the two days, Jesus announces his decision to go back to Judea. The normal reaction of the disciples, pointing out the peril involved, serves to give Jesus the opportunity to explain what guides his life. He must work during the twelve hours of sunlight; those who work at night stumble. As noticed in a previous meditation, his life follows a schedule that is well established. The disciples may think that the threats to stone him make the present a dark time. They are wrong. While he is in the world it is daylight. After having clarified that he moves about during the twelve hours of daylight, Jesus announces why he is going back to Judea and for what purpose: "Our friend Lazarus has fallen asleep but I go to wake him out of sleep" (11:11). As readers of this gospel have learned to expect by now, the disciples fail to understand Jesus' words. To make sure his readers understand and to give them the clue to the story, the narrator explains that by "sleep" Jesus was not referring to "rest in sleep" but to "death" (11:13). In the process readers are also told that as believers they should think of biological death as "sleep."

Working under a misunderstanding of Jesus' words, Thomas now encourages his fellow disciples to go to Judea with Jesus "that we may die with him" (11:16). Jesus has already said twice what is actually taking place. In response to the news of Lazarus' illness, Jesus said: "This illness is not unto death; it is for the glory of God, so that the Son of God may be glorified by means of it" (11:4). Then he said that he was going to Judea to wake Lazarus out of his sleep. Thomas has failed to understand both declarations. His demonstration of loyalty is admirable, but his misunderstanding is an ironic twist aimed at making sure readers understand.

Transjordan is the backdrop for the first act, where the major themes of the drama are announced: When people think that it is a dark, perilous time they must know that when Jesus is with them it is daytime, a time to do one's work. What is about to happen will bring about the glorification of the Son, who thereby brings glory to God. The purpose of the Son in the world is to wake people out of their death.

Once back in Judea, as Jesus comes close to Bethany, we are told that Lazarus' body has already been in a tomb four days. Mary and Martha are in mourning and many of "the Jews" are at their home consoling them. News that Jesus is approaching causes Martha to go out to meet him at the edge of the village. She greets him with a reproach: "Lord, if you had been here my brother would not have died. Even now I know that whatever you ask from God, God will give you" (11:21 - 22). With these words Martha expresses not only disappointment, but also expectation. Something about Jesus transcends her frustration and sets up expectations: in her mind God gives Jesus whatever he asks.

Jesus' words of comfort, "Your brother will rise again" are interpreted by Martha in a familiar apocalyptic context. She is confident of God's justice and that her brother will rise again at the resurrection of the just on the last day. To correct this affirmation of traditional apocalyptic doctrine, Jesus delivers the central affirmation of the gospel *According to John*: "I am the resurrection and the life; he who believes in me though he die yet shall he live, and whoever lives and believes in me, shall never die" (11:25 – 26).

The word "die" in this declaration is used twice with contrasting meanings, something we should not be surprised to find here; the reader who overlooks the double meaning of words may never understand this gospel. Anyone who believes and dies, dies biologically. Anyone who lives and believes will never die eschatologically. The narrator has already advised us that by sleep Jesus was referring to biological death. With this clue we see that Jesus' words are telling us that he who believes in him as the One Sent by the Father may die biologically, but will never die eschatologically. The reason is that Jesus is the resurrection and the life, that is, eschatological life. In other words, the resurrection is not to be waited for in a last day, as Martha thinks. Eternal life, which is the essence of the resurrection, is available here now to all who believe that Jesus, as Martha confesses, is "the Son of God, he who is coming into the world" (11:27).

After this illuminating dialogue, Martha goes back home and tells Mary, "The Teacher is here and is calling for you" (11:28). Mary immediately leaves for the outskirts of the village where Jesus had been talking with Martha. "The Jews" who were at the house now follow after Mary. Meeting Jesus, Mary repeats Martha's reproach word for word. Mary and "the Jews" are not aware of the conversation Jesus had with Martha, and when they approach Jesus they are all weeping. To this emotional demonstration of sorrow, Jesus reacts with an outburst of anger. What translators render as "he was deeply moved in the Spirit and troubled" (11:33), should not be understood to mean that he joined them in their sorrow. The first Greek word used expresses indignation, censure, strong disagreement, and the second means to be agitated, to be dismayed. His visceral reaction was not of sympathy but of repulsion. Their inability to understand why he had come frustrated him.

That he was vehemently agitated and dismayed seems to demonstrate Jesus' humanity, but not necessarily. God in the Scriptures is often given anthropomorphic qualities. God flares in anger, or repents from having done something. That Jesus became deeply dismayed does not demonstrate his sympathy for those who sorrow because of the power of death. It was a vehement demonstration of frustration and impatience with those who could not understand what he had come to do. He had not come too late, as the two sisters thought. He had come at the right time to manifest the glory of God. He was not going to engage in a conversation with those who mourned and wept. In the synoptic stories, by contrast, Jesus tells both the widow of Nain and those in Jairus' house "Do not weep" (Lk. 8:13; Mk. 5:39; Lk. 8:52). In the case of Lazarus, the time to do what needed to be done had come. He now asked: "Where have you laid him?" They all answered, "Come and see."

The request to come and see appears in other contexts in this gospel as an invitation to believe. In this instance it functions in reverse, as an invitation so see the realm of biological death and the smelly decomposition of a body. It is at this juncture that the narrator reports that Jesus wept. Does this mean that he has succumbed after all to the powerful sorrowing of those about him? Is he showing his human sympathy when confronted with death? Is this the Johannine equivalent to the synoptic description of Jesus' anguish at Gethsemane? Is Jesus commiserating with the tragedy of the human condition? Did Jesus weep because the one thing certain about women and men is that they all die? The answer to these questions is given by the reaction of "the Jews." They have been brought into the story for this comment: "See how he loved him" (11:36). If anyone thinks that he is weeping for the loss of a loved one, just like Mary and they were, one has not yet come to terms with Johannine irony. He is not weeping to show his love. He is weeping out of frustration with those who cannot discern the reason for his coming to Bethany.

The story continues, "Then Jesus deeply moved again, came to the tomb" (11:38). That is to say, he came to the tomb totally dismayed, frustrated, annoyed. The report that Jesus wept is sandwiched by the two reports of his emotional outburst of consternation and indignation. Martha, Mary and now "the Jews" that were there (11:37) have expressed their displeasure with Jesus for not having prevented Lazarus' death. Jesus is reacting to their inability to see. Rather than telling him "come and see" death, they should have been seeing life in him. The two outbursts of visceral emotion that mark this scene and the melodramatic comment of "the Jews," indicate that Jesus has become very upset. Laughter and tears are often signs of nervousness which itself can have many different causes. "Jesus wept" is the reaction to the invitation to "come and see." The irony of the situation is that both the invitation and the reaction must be seen upside down. That Jesus wept does demonstrate his humanity, but they were not tears of sorrow. They were tears of consternation.

After the first act in Transjordan, and the second act at the outskirts of Bethany, we are ready for the drama's third act.

The tomb was a cave whose entrance was covered by a stone. Normally a tomb like this was a cave on the side of a steep hill. A flat vertical surface had been made on the hill, and the stone that served as a door to the cave was a large stone carved as a wheel that could be rolled on a stone pavement and a small wall that created a groove that prevented the stone wheel from separating from the face of the tomb on the now flat vertical surface on the hill. Jesus now asked for the stone to be rolled. Like the disciples who had warned Jesus of the consequences of a return to Judea, Martha warns Jesus of the consequences of opening the tomb. According to the narrative, Jesus now reminds Martha of something he had not told her. To Martha he had said that he who believes would never die. He now claims to have told her "if you would believe you would see the glory of God" (11:40). We may recall that to the disciples in Transjordan he had said that Lazarus' illness was "for the glory of God, so that the Son of God may be glorified by means of it" (11:4). It would seem that what Jesus claims to have told Martha serves as counterpoint to the invitation to come and see where Lazarus was buried. Thus, Jesus tells Martha now that he who believes will *see* the glory of God. Believing, seeing, and the glory of God are available to human beings. On the basis of this promise, the stone blocking the entrance to the tomb is rolled to one side.

Now the theme announced in the dialogue with Martha comes to the fore, but with a twist. Martha had said, "I know that whatever you ask from God, God will give you" (11:22). Jesus now prays, but he does not ask a thing from God. Rather, he thanks God for having heard him, as God always hears him (11:41). Then he explains that this prayer is not for God's or his benefit. It is for the benefit of "the people standing by, that they may believe that thou didst send me" (11:42). What needs to be believed is not that he is the Christ, or the Son of God, the King of Israel, or the Son of man. It is that he is the One Sent by God. Eternal life, resurrection, victory over eschatological death, is to be had by those who believe that he came from God. This is the gospel in a nutshell.

Having established that, Jesus cried out, "Lazarus, come out." When the dead man came out, his hands and feet bound and his face covered, Jesus said, "Unbind him, and let him go" (11:44).

The picture of Lazarus bound and yet coming out of the tomb is the iconic representation of the powerlessness of death. It is the proof of the effectiveness of Jesus' word: "He who believes in me, though he die, yet shall he live, and whoever lives and believes in me shall never die" (11:25 – 26).

Like all miracle stories in the gospels this one also ends with a notice of the crowd's reaction. In this case, however, it follows the Johannine pattern. The word of Jesus creates a crisis that divides the audience. The narrator reports: "Many of the Jews therefore, who had come with Mary and had seen what he did, believed in him; but some of them went to the Pharisees and told them what Jesus had done" (11:45 – 46). And on that very day "they took counsel how to put him to death" (11:53).

The story of the raising of Lazarus is the encapsulation of the gospel *According to John*. Apocalypticism emerged to affirm that even though at present God's retributive justice seems not to be working, it will be effective on the last day. *According to John* affirms that even though it is true that God is a God of justice, he is primarily a God of life. Early in this story we were told that Jesus loved Martha and her sister and Lazarus, but at the beginning of the gospel we were told that "God so loved the world that he gave his only Son that whoever believes in him should not perish but have eternal life. For God sent the Son into the world, not to condemn [judge] the world, but that the world might be saved through him" (3:16 – 17). Believers don't live in the apocalyptic darkness of a stormy sea that threatens to engulf and sink them in its depths. They live in the light which, as the prologue says, is the life of the world (1:4). They live unbound, free in the knowledge that the Father loves them and sent the Son to give them eternal life in this world now. That is the truth of the Gospel that makes women and men free. "If the Son makes you free, you shall be free indeed" (8:36). Ultimate freedom is confidence that eschatological death has been conquered, and biological death is a sleep. Whoever knows this truth is free (8:32) and has been unbound and let go. The truth of the gospel is not found in esoteric knowledge but in eternal life. The freedom of the Gospel is the freedom to live by the call of the One who is the Resurrection and the Life.

22
Rivers of Living Water

Water is indispensable for life. There are organisms which require a very small quantity, but no matter how they are constituted, they need water to live. In the most arid desert, under the surface, there are living things which retain water and use it with amazing economy. They also would die if they lacked water. It is not by chance that the explorations which are now taking place on the planet Mars consider it a priority to determine whether water ever existed there. The reason is obvious. Water is the *sine qua non* for life in the physical world. On Sept. 27, 2012, the scientists conducting the exploration of Mars announced that they have received pictures of stones rounded by their movement under the force of the current of a stream. What millions of years ago was a stream, however, is now a dry bed.

That water is essential was already recognized in the ancient world. Most of the pre-scientific stories of creation begin with a primordial ocean as the original reality that had to be subjugated for the creation of the world in which we live. This is the case also in Genesis 1 where the narrative begins with "and the Spirit of God was moving over the face of the waters" (Gen. 1:1). In Genesis 2 the garden that God planted in the primordial desert could become a reality because of the river with four branches that gave it life (Gen. 2:10). The description of the new earth in Revelation, which enumerates the basic elements of the story of Genesis 2, includes the river of life (Rev. 22:1). In the vision of a restored Jerusalem received by Ezekiel, the small stream of water that flows from under the altar in the temple eventually becomes a powerful river of life to the nations (Ez. 47:1 – 12). In these visions life with God will be sustained also by water.

These richly allusive descriptions of water provide the background for the references to water that illumine the theology of *According to John*. To start, we note that in this gospel the baptism of John the Baptist is explicitly contrasted with Jesus' baptism of water and spirit. In the baptism of John water functions as the purifier of sins. As such, his baptism is a rite of purification. By contrast, the water of the baptism of Jesus establishes a new life. The baptism of water and spirit engenders sons of God. To be noted is that the contrast between the two baptisms is not that one is "of water" and the other is of the Spirit. The baptism of Jesus that engenders sons of God is "of water and the Spirit" (3:5).

The water of the baptism of Jesus, however, remains undefined. No discrete explanation is given of the water that serves as a vehicle of the Spirit. What is it that distinguishes it from the water of the baptism of John the Baptist? This obfuscation is somewhat disconcerting because in this gospel we are told that Jesus baptized more disciples than John (4:1). No doubt the narrator wished to establish a distinction between the two waters, but fails to make it. Apparently he has something up his sleeve.

Something similar occurs in the scene of Jesus and the Samaritan woman. The Samaritans depend on the water of the well Jacob dug to provide for the needs of his family and his cattle (4:12). This is a water source that has supplied the physical needs of people and cattle for about seventeen centuries. In all this time no one has ever been disappointed by coming to it in search of water and finding it dry. This water source has given life to multiple generations. The well dug by Jacob has been a fountain of life whose effectiveness through time is undeniable.

The water of the well of Jacob is characterized by only one of its properties: its capacity to quench thirst is temporary. Those who drink this water become thirsty again. By contrast, Jesus promises that the water he will provide will quench forever the thirst of whoever drinks it (4:13 – 14). What surprises us is that when the Samaritan woman anxiously asks: "Sir, give me this water that I may not thirst, nor come here to draw" (4:15), instead of giving her the promised water Jesus changes the subject. Again the reader is left wondering about Jesus' water.

The report of the wedding feast at Cana mentions that in the house of the feast's host "six stone jars were standing there, for the Jewish rites of purification, each holding twenty or thirty gallons" (2:6). In contrast to the water of the well which Jacob dug "and drank from it himself, and his sons, and his cattle" (4:12), the water of the stone jars in the house where a wedding was celebrated in Cana of Galilee was not water for daily use, to quench thirst. This was water for purification rites which "the Jews" had to perform periodically according to the rules of the case. One of the rules was that the water for purifications could not come from a cistern or a pool. It had to be water that had been moving in a current – that is, "living" water. That is why the six stone jars were empty. They were filled when purification rites were to be carried out.

The water of the baptism of John, the water of Jacob's well, and the water with which the stone jars of a house in Cana were filled symbolize religion at the formal level, at the level of traditional and prescribed rites that have sustained a people in a relationship with God. As a formal institution with its traditions through generations religion has, for many, quenched the thirst for God. As such it merits gratitude and recognition.

The presence of the Son of God in the world, however, has transformed the situation. Water has become wine, and the wine provided by the Son is not just the common wine that is served when the guests have been drinking freely and have lost the capacity to assess the quality of what they are drinking. Wine experts, in full use of their faculties, have declared it the best wine they ever drank. The wine that takes the place of the water is not only effective as a thirst quencher. It is indispensable in a feast where people are not just living, especially at a wedding feast that celebrates that two people are going to experience the fullness of life.

As argued in previous meditations, *According to John* does not share the apocalyptic perspective that informs the ministry of Jesus in *According to Mark*, and that *According to Matthew* and *According to Luke* adopt with modifications peculiar to each. In *According to John* the scene of Jesus' calming the storm in the Sea of Galilee is told with rather significant modifications. The scene is an echo of the stories of creation in which the creator imposes his will over the primordial sea. It is only in the gospels that the Lake of Genesareth is known as the Sea of Galilee. As a body of water this "sea" is not much bigger than the small interior lakes of the state of Michigan in which I reside. To the evangelists it is a "sea" for theological reasons. The sea represents the primordial waters that are the source of the powers that oppose God's purposes and must be subdued before creation can take place. In the visions of *Daniel* the political powers that persecute the people of God are represented by mythological beasts that come out of the sea. The vision of *Revelation* says there will be no sea in the new earth (Rev. 21:1). Surely the early Christians understood that the representation of Jesus' walking on the sea and imposing his will against its fury announces the triumph of life over the chaotic forces of death.

According to John draws a dramatic scene in which Jesus makes himself known for the first time as "I am" (6:20). In this scene Jesus walks over the stormy sea, the source of anxiety and fear. The one who walks over the water of the sea is the resurrection and the life, the one who triumphs over the powers of evil and death that intend to separate the creatures from their Creator. Water not only can represent religion as an institution that is partially effective since it quenches thirst temporarily; it can also represent the source of demonic power that rise with force to smother life itself in the claws of death. The image of Jesus as the sovereign over the sea is full of power and hope.

The central, decisive scene in *According to John* is the appearance of Jesus at the final day of the Feast of Tabernacles. The atmosphere for the scene is charged because Jesus is already a marked man; it looks as if Jesus is not going to attend the feast because his hour has not yet come (7:6, 8). During the first days of the feast there is great curiosity on the part of the multitude as to whether Jesus will come or not. Jesus' brothers criticize him for not making himself known, and the multitude would like to come to a conclusion as to whether he is genuine or a charlatan (7:12). However, "for fear of the Jews" the people were not expressing their desire to make up their minds about him (7:13). Their doubts and expectations are resolved "about the middle of the feast" when Jesus not only comes to Jerusalem but spends the day teaching at the temple (7:14).

The Feast of Tabernacles, or of Booths, lasts seven days and commemorates the providence of God when the people wandered in the desert after the exodus from Egypt. The most necessary thing in that inhospitable wasteland was water. In those trying days God provided a rock that supplied their need for water. On the last great day of the feast the priests and the people descended to the pool of Siloam and filled their jars with water. Then they climbed to the court of the temple and poured the water in their jars on the altar. This made the water run from the altar through the court of the gentiles and eventually drop down the hill to the valley of Kidron. In this way the feast not only commemorated the water supplied by the rock in the desert, but also anticipated the fulfillment of the vision of Ezekiel about the stream of water that flowed from below the altar of the temple (Ez. 47:1).

While the priests and the people are enacting the dramatic flow of water from the altar, Jesus proclaims himself the fountain of the water of life: "If any one thirst, let him come to me, and let him who believes in me drink." The basis for the proclamation is a quote from Scripture: "Out of his guts (*koilías* = cavity, entrails) shall flow rivers of living water" (7:37 – 38, my translation).

Early in his conversation with the Samaritan woman, Jesus said to her that if she knew with whom she was speaking, she would be asking him for water, "and he would have given you living water" (4:10). But his answer did not try to distinguish the water of a well from water that moves in a current. The living water Jesus offers the Samaritan at the well of Jacob is of another order. It is the water that flows with the wine of his blood.

All the references to the "living water" that Jesus offers when his hour had not yet come (2:4, 23; 7:8) point to the water Jesus provides when his hour *had* come (13:1). His living water also flows from the rock, but it flows with blood. Just as Moses struck the rock and water flowed from it to give life to the people that wandered in the desert (Ex. 17:6; Num. 20:10 – 13), a Roman soldier struck the already dead body (a rock) of Jesus on the cross, and from him flowed the blood and water that gives life to the people who believe in him (19:34). All the references to living water in the gospel find their referent in this scene.

The text of Scripture that predicts that from his guts would flow rivers of living water has not been found. The reference could be to Isaiah 12:3: "With joy you will draw water from the wells of salvation." It could be to Jeremiah 2:13: "For my people have committed two evils: they have forsaken me, the fountain of living waters, and hewed out cisterns for themselves, broken cisterns, that can hold no water," or to Jeremiah 17:13: "they have forsaken the Lord, the fountain of living water." The poetic references to the rock of Horeb speak of the abundance of water provided by God in the desert: "He made streams come out of the rock, and caused waters to flow down like rivers … He opened the rock, and water gushed forth; it flowed through the desert like a river" (Ps. 78:16, 20). The water of the fountain of salvation is the water of the Rock of Calvary, and Jesus promised that all those who drink it will never thirst again. In the Johannine perspective, living water does not flow from the altar of the temple in Jerusalem which both Ezekiel and John the Theologian saw in vision. It flows from the rock of the temple that is the body (2:21) of the one who, like the serpent that Moses lifted up in the desert, has been lifted up so that every one who believes in him may have eternal life (3:15). This is the water that Jesus offered to the Samaritan woman and to all the participants at the Feast of Tabernacles, and that *According to John* offers to all those who read it. This is not the water of the baptism of John the Baptist or of religion at the level of sacramental rites, but the water that flows with the wine/blood of life in the Spirit.

The dependence of life on water has been recognized throughout history. As such, its power as the giver of life is indisputable. As a symbol of God's providential gift to creation, and at the same time the source of the powers that challenge God's rule over creation, it has no rival. *According to John* most creatively taps the rich allusive overtones of water to highlight the new age of the Spirit, as explicitly pointed out by the narrator in reference to Jesus' proclamation at the Feast of Tabernacles (7:39). The living water that Jesus freely gives is the water of the baptism of water and Spirit. Those who receive this baptism are born of God; in their daily life they manifest the triumph of God within creation. *According to John* ties the living water to the baptism of the Spirit and to the blood of the cross, thereby democratizing the community of Christians – all are equally dependent on the Spirit for life. In the process it also tells us that life in the Spirit is not detached from material realities, like blood, wine and water. The gospel does not spiritualize the Christian life into an other-worldly existence. The very materialistic vision of the reign of God which Ezekiel described in terms of the river that flows from under the altar in the court of the temple of Jerusalem has only been transferred to the new temple of the body of the glorified Son of man. The river of living water is already giving life to the world.

23

WHERE ARE YOU FROM?

To the surprise of many, *According to John* exhibits elements characteristic of docetism. This doctrine says that the disciples saw Jesus alive after his crucifixion because the *Logos* who became incarnate was a divine being and therefore did not suffer death. In other words, it was not the mission of the *Logos* to die as an expiatory sacrifice, but to reveal to human beings the way of salvation. His saving mission did not require death and resurrection. In this gospel Jesus is presented as a divine being, and his teaching points out how to obtain eternal life. Thus, Jesus' teachings brings out spiritual realities using a dualistic language with strong philosophical reverberations. From the very beginning of the narrative, without making a reference to his birth, it is proclaimed that the protagonist has been with God since "the beginning" and is in fact God.

These connections with docetism, however, are somewhat in tension with the important role played by the account of the death of Jesus and by the role played by "the prince of this world" in this gospel. Most important in this regard is the presentation of the Risen Lord living in the body of the crucified Jesus. This is in contrast with the *Gospel of Thomas* and *"Q"* (a source used by the authors of *According to Matthew* and *According to Luke*), which contain only teachings of Jesus with very little circumstantial information and do not include his passion and death or references to his resurrection.

According to John has a detailed account of the capture, trial and crucifixion of Jesus. This counteracts its docetic aspects. However, there are notable differences with the Synoptic narratives. There is no account of hours of anguish at the Garden of Gethsemane. In the face of the mob that is searching for him, Jesus is in control of the situation, and when he identifies himself saying, "I am he," those who had come to take him prisoner fall flat on their backs to the ground (18:6). Judas does not betray him with a kiss. Jesus' divinity is never in doubt, and death is not seen by him as the enemy that needs to be defeated.

In the judgment before Pilate, when Pilate aims to put him in his place by reminding him that he has power of life and death over him, Jesus corrects him pointing out that his power as a Roman procurator is derived from the power that comes from God, that is, from him (19:11). On the cross Jesus does not cite Psalm 22 as the key with which to interpret his death, as in *According to Mark*. The psalm brings out that the one who feels abandoned by a god who does not do justice ends up proclaiming that God does indeed do justice and has carried out the promised salvation (Ps. 22:27 – 31). In *According to John* Jesus on the cross proclaims, "It is finished [done]" (19:30). What was expected of him has been accomplished before his death. That is, his death is not the means of his triumph, but the final point of his "work." His death is the "sign" that must be seen by all and is his return to the Father. He does not face it as the enemy. It is a tool with which he accomplishes his purpose.

In *According to Mark,* in the trial before Caiaphas several witnesses bring forth contradictory accusations which fail to justify Jesus' condemnation (Mk. 14:58 – 60). This causes Caiaphas, somewhat annoyed, to ask him a pointed question: "Are you the Christ, the Son of the Blessed?" (Mk.14:61). To this question Jesus gives a straight answer: "I am" (Mk. 14:62). With this Caiaphas has obtained what he wanted: Jesus is guilty of blasphemy (Mk. 14:64). By contrast, in *According to John* the High Priest asks Jesus "about his disciples and his teaching" (18:19). Jesus avoids the question pointing out that this should be asked of those who heard him at the temple, the synagogue and other public places. Frustrated and without a definite charge against Jesus, the High Priest sends him to be judged by Pilate. The Roman procurator asks those who bring Jesus to him the obvious question: "What accusation do you bring against this man?" (18:29). Incapable of identifying an accusation, "the Jews" admit that they do not have a definite charge by saying that Pilate may be sure that they are not bringing to him an innocent man (18:30).

This stratagem serves to establish that "the Jews" are seeking a death sentence from Pilate against a man who is not, as they say, an evildoer. When Pilate tells them to judge him according to "your own law," they say: "It is not lawful for us to put any man to death" (18:32). The narrator then explains that it was necessary for Jesus to die at the hands of the Romans to fulfill the prophecy that he would die "lifted up" (12:32), that is, crucified. Under Jewish law he would have died stoned, like Stephen. In other words, his death is to be a "lifting up" because its function is to be the ascent to the Father.

The narration of the trial of Jesus in *According to John* is built on four questions asked by Pilate. They are organically structured on the theology of this gospel. The first question is: "Are you the King of the Jews?" (18:33). Jesus avoids this question by asking Pilate how he came to think that. Twice in this gospel Jesus has been seen as a king. Only *According to John* says that after the feeding of the five thousand there arose a desire among some in the crowd to crown him king (6:15). Jesus, aware of what is going on, succeeds in getting away to the mountain to pray alone. Later, when Jesus is arriving at Jerusalem, a multitude comes out of the city with palm branches and enters the city with him proclaiming, "Blessed is he who comes in the name of the Lord, even the King of Israel" (12:13, citing Zach. 9:9). This time the reaction of Jesus is to seat himself on a young ass, thus making clear that, in fact, he is not a king. The colt of an ass, apparently, happened to have been there. This is quite different from the story in *According to Mark*, where Jesus sends disciples to bring "a colt on which no one has ever sat" to him (Mk. 11:2 – 3), that is a young, untrained gelding.

In this connection it is necessary to note that in *According to John* Jesus is not identified as the son of David. Popular opinion has it that he is a native of Nazareth. Since it is expected that the Messiah is to be a descendant of David born in Bethlehem, Jesus does not meet these requirements. As far as the narrator of *According to John* is concerned, those who disqualify him on account of his Galilean origin and his non-Davidic lineage are correct (7:41 – 42). This means that a royal connection and messianic expectations as a justification of his death are being explicitly disallowed.

Pilate answers Jesus' question as to the origin of his thinking of him as a king with another question, his second one: "Am I a Jew?" (18:35). Pilate's question seems to be asking for a rhetorical sparring. It may be his way of showing annoyance at Jesus' question. Everyone knows that Pontius Pilate is a Roman installed as procurator of Judea by Emperor Tiberius. Whether Pilate is or is not a Jew seems to have nothing to do with whether or not Jesus is the King of the Jews. Are only Jews able to identify the King of the Jews?

Of course, the original question "Are you the King of the Jews?" must be understood in context. The "Jews" affirm that they are bringing an evildoer to be sentenced to death. If Jesus admits to being the King of the Jews he will be accused of sedition. But in the context of *According to John* such admission is not possible. Jesus explains himself saying, "My kingdom is not of this world" (18:36). As already noticed, he does not meet the Jewish expectation of a Messiah who is a Son of David. His presence in this world has nothing to do with the kings and kingdoms of this world. Jesus came "to bear witness to the truth" (18:37). Political power and ultimate truth are realities of different universes. In the political world justice and truth are often the first victims. Those who belong to the world "below," the realm of the flesh, fail to distinguish between the "above" and the "below" (8:23). No, Pilate is not a Jew, but this is not due to his belonging to a different genetic line, or to another political reality. He is not "a Jew" because he is not boxed in by a religious ideology that defines things according to unquestionable preconceptions. He is not "a Jew" because he is interested in establishing a valid charge against the prisoner. On the other hand, he is "a Jew" because he cannot understand spiritual realities, seeing things only from the perspective of the world "below." Pilate's rhetorical question only serves to cast him, the central figure in Jesus' crucifixion, as one not up to his responsibilities.

Not knowing where he fits, Pilate makes his third question: "What is truth?" (18:38). This question is more ironic than the previous one, but also quite revealing. How can anyone pose this question to the one who is the Truth? Pilate's question is not dismissive. It reflects his confusion. On the one hand, he is trying to establish a legitimate accusation against a prisoner brought to him as an evildoer. On the other, he is unable to form an opinion of the accused. Is he willing to face the Truth? Until now Pilate has been conducting himself correctly. His motives are honorable; but is he willing to be born "from above" in order to see? From the perspective of the world "below," Pilate insists three times that he does not find a crime in him (18:38; 19:4, 6).

Fearing they will not achieve their goal, "the Jews," who had rejected the offer to judge him by their "own law," now declare that "we have a law, and by that law he ought to die, because he has made himself the Son of God" (19:7). The accusation now is not that he is a seditious person but that he is a blasphemer. Pilate's reaction to this information is surprising. The accusation that Jesus wishes to be the King of the Jews has been set aside because Jesus denies an earthly kingdom. Pilate, as a good politician, does not see a connection between a king of another world and a witness to the truth. Considering the possibility that Jesus may be the Son of God, something that Jesus has claimed publicly throughout his life, Pilate has become disoriented. He who moments earlier threatened the prisoner with life and death power over him is now wondering about the significance of the new accusation.

At the end of his wits, Pilate asks his fourth question: "Where are you from?" (19:9). Finally Pilate has asked the decisive question. This is the question the narrator has been building toward, the question that drives the plot of the whole gospel, the question every reader of *According to John* must answer. The correct answer to this question is the central Truth of *According to John*. Life and death depend on it.

At the beginning of the gospel, Philip tells Nathanael that he has found "him of whom Moses in the law and also the prophets wrote" (1:46). Nathanael reacts saying that nothing good can come from Nazareth. Ironically, Nathanael is right and Philip is poorly informed. Without a doubt nothing good comes out of Nazareth, but Jesus is not from Nazareth. He is from "above." This is what all women and men must come to understand. The gospel begins and ends emphasizing that the most important thing to know about Jesus is to know where he is from. In his arguments with "the Jews" and in his prayer to the Father, Jesus insists that the purpose of his life on earth is to cause humanity to recognize him as the One who descended from "above," the One sent by the Father (11:42; 16:27, 30; 17:3). To affirm this makes clear that one knows where Jesus is from. "The Jews," on the other hand, openly admit "we know not where he comes from" (9:29).

He who has no patience to face the Truth asks: "What is truth?" The frustration and anxiety of the one asking the question demonstrate that he does not have the capacity to recognize the One before him. Foolishly Pilate presents him to the people proclaiming, "Here is the man" (19:5), but he is not a man from "below." Only those "born from above" can recognize the One Sent by the Father. This declaration of Pilate, however, is full of irony. While revealing the inability of Pilate to recognize Jesus' true origin, it also declares a basic truth of this gospel: the Son of the Father who descended from heaven is actually a man. The incarnation is the central paradox at the heart of the Truth. Like the High Priest who counsels expediency advising that it is better for one man to die than for the whole nation to be destroyed (11:50), Pilate without realizing is affirming the incarnation. Rather than giving the people their man, he has presented to them, in the eyes of the narrator, with the Truth who is a Man. This affirmation and the notation that after Jesus' death a soldier opened a wound on his side with his spear "and at once came out blood and water" (19:34, the blood [the life of man] and the water [the life of the Spirit]) are the ultimate pictures of the reality of the incarnation.

The narration of the trial of Jesus gives the impression that Pilate has failed in his attempt to find a legitimate cause to declare him guilty of a crime that would justify his crucifixion. Three times he declares to have found no crime in him. Naturally, under the circumstances, Pilate is going to set free the prisoner against whom he has been unable to find a reasonable accusation. Blasphemy is not a chargeable offense under Roman law. At the time of the Punic Wars (264 – 146 BCE), afraid of a Carthaginian victory, the Roman senate opened the doors to Eastern mystery religions and gave them civil rights. Followers of these cults were able to follow their rites and customs. Eventually Judaism also became a legally recognized religion (a *religio licita*). Blasphemy could be a legitimate charge only under Jewish law.

Realizing that Pilate is not going to satisfy their wishes, "the Jews" opt for a personal attack against Pilate, but their maneuver only serves the theological agenda of the gospel. Threatening Pilate with *lése majesté* (insulting the king), they proclaim not to consider God their king. Caesar is their king. With this declaration "the Jews" of *According to John* are placed in a worse light than "the Jews" of *According to Matthew* who demand that "his blood be on us and our children" (Mt. 17:25). By confessing that Caesar, rather than God, is their king, "the Jews" who demand the crucifixion of Jesus confess to being apostates from the religion of Moses and the prophets. The irony of the situation could not be missed by the original readers.

The final irony in this story is the scene of "the Jews" asking Pilate to change the title he has placed on the cross of Jesus. It reads: "Jesus of Nazareth: the King of the Jews" (19:19). Since Caesar is their king, they want to make sure that nobody thinks they consider the one hanging from a cross their king. Pilate denies their request. On political matters Pilate sees clearly through their hypocrisy. To reaffirm in the strongest form possible what he has proclaimed in Hebrew, Greek and Latin (19:20) Pilate says: "*Ho gégrafa, gégrafa*," "What I have written, I have written" (19:22). In Greek the verb in the perfect tense transcends time. In other words, Pilate tells "the Jews," "You can say what you want, but officially Jesus of Nazareth is your king." The real irony is that having rejected the One Sent by the Father from above and having chosen Caesar as their king, those who wished to have Pilate declare Jesus a criminal are condemned by Pilate to have the man from Nazareth, rather than Caesar, as their king. The one who dies on the cross as the King of the Jews, proclaimed as such in three main languages of the Mediterranean world, has been "lifted up" at the insistence of "the Jews" and thereby draws all human beings to himself (12:32). In the process, "the Jews" are being given the definitive Johannine characterization: they rejected God as their king.

According to John gives singular importance to the crucifixion, but narrates it and the trial of Jesus with its theological agenda on the surface. From the very beginning it directs the attention of its readers to the outpouring of the Spirit that flows from the entrails of the One who has been lifted up and wounded, thus opening the way for all human beings to access the world "above." Anxious that not one of his readers should miss his purpose, the narrator finishes his presentation of the trial and crucifixion saying: "He who saw it has borne witness – his testimony is true, and he knows that he tells the truth – that you also may believe" (19:35). The whole gospel finds its goal in this scene at the cross. No one has ascended to heaven, except the one who descended (3:13) and opened the way so that all those who believe in Him may have the world above opened to them, and the Father and the Son abiding in them. His crucifixion is his ascent, his return to where he is from. It is the fulfillment of the promise made to Nathanael: the Son of man as the ladder that makes access and exchanges with heaven possible. This narration gives the death of Jesus a very definite function within the symbolic universe of the descent and ascent of the Son sent by the Father to give life to the world. For this reason, during his ministry Jesus could refer to his death as his glorification. Thus, the nuances of the narrative give to the gospel's tacit docetism a thorough revision.

24
ABIDE IN MY LOVE

The gospel *According to John* is a fascinating document. There is little doubt that of the four gospels, it is the one that since antiquity has inspired Christians the most. *According to Mark* has Jesus moving at a fast pace, facing demons, exorcising them and announcing the destruction of Jerusalem and the imminent coming of the Son of man in glory. *According to Matthew*, with the Sermon on the Mount and the promise that Jesus is always present among his disciples, has informed Christian norms of conduct through the centuries. *According to Luke* and *Acts of the Apostles* trace the advance of the kingdom of God from Galilee to Jerusalem and from Jerusalem to Rome, demonstrating that God has a plan that is being accomplished in history. *According to John* is the gospel that has inspired Christians to see Jesus as the One Sent by the Father to give to all human beings access to eternal life. *According to John* puts the world of the Spirit that gives life at the disposal of all its readers.

Moreover, what makes *According to John* fascinating is its simple language. This aspect, however, is deceiving. The reader who does not take note of the different levels in which words have meaning does not get the full rhetorical impact of its message. In previous meditations I have already directed attention to the use of irony and of words with double meanings, with specified meanings, or with multiple meanings. The semantic richness of its vocabulary is evident especially in the verbs. For example, I have noted how "to lift up," "to glorify" and "to crucify" are used indiscriminately to refer to the Son's return journey to the Father.

To elaborate further on this aspect of the gospel I will call attention to the way in which some verbs are used to shape a well conceived theological framework. To begin with, let us note references to the verb "to hear." I have previously emphasized that this gospel, more than any other, presupposes good knowledge of the Old Testament. In Hebrew "to hear" is *shamea*. This word means both "to hear" and "to obey." That is, he who hears, obeys. He who does not obey has his ears plugged up and does not hear. He who does not obey has "a stiff neck." He cannot turn his head from one side to the other to take directions. In Hebrew it is understood that those who hear, *act* on the basis of what they heard. He who hears and does not obey, has not heard. As is commonly said, it went "in one ear and out the other." The message made no impact on the person.

This characteristic of the Hebrew language is evident in the use of the verb "to hear" in *According to John*. For example, "Why do you not understand what I say? It is because you cannot bear to hear my word" (8:43). "Every one who is of the truth hears my voice" (18:37). "My sheep hear my voice, and I know them, and they follow me" (10:27). Finally, "Everyone who has heard and learned from the Father comes to me" (6:45). He who hears, comes. He who does not come has not heard. Or, as Jesus explains, "the Jews" do not come to him because they think that what Jesus is offering them is to be found in a different source.

In one of his most severe indictments Jesus says that the problem of "the Jews" is that they search for eternal life in the Scriptures. But to attain to eternal life they have "to come to me" (5:39). On another occasion Jesus says: "He who comes to me shall not hunger," and the parallel sentence explains: "he who believes in me shall never thirst" (6:35). "To come" is "to believe." Referring to certain Jews who had witnessed the resurrection of Lazarus, the narrator uses the following verbal sequence: "Many of the Jews therefore, who had *come* with Mary and had *seen* what he did, *believed* in him" (11:45).

To hear and to come results in seeing, and those who see become witnesses. In the prologue the Johannine community confesses: "we have beheld his glory" (1:14). John the Baptist proclaims: "I have seen and have born witness" (1:34). On the other hand, "the Jews" ask: "What sign do you do, that we may see, and believe you?" (6:30). Their apparent interest in Jesus' claims, however, is not considered sincere by Jesus. Their use of the Scriptures to declare Jesus a sinner reveals that they are blind, in spite of the certainty with which they claim to have good sight. They are not different from those with plugged ears. Jesus reinforces this by declaring: "For judgment I came into this world, that those who do not see may see, and that those who see may become blind" (9:39). In other words, he came to transform the senses and equip them to recognize the work of God, that is, equip them to believe. In this context, and in marked contrast with the request of "the Jews" for a sign, the request of the Greeks is sincere, "Sir, we wish to see Jesus" (12:21). These Greeks, who disappear as soon as they have delivered their scripted lines, are the ones who need Jesus to confront his destiny. Their request establishes that his hour has come (12:23, 27).

Those who wish to see must have a definite object on which to focus their sight. The sign that "the Jews" asked for with dubious intentions and the Greeks asked for with utmost sincerity had to be made available. Jesus had to be "lifted up." On the cross faith finds the object that justifies it. As Jesus says: "He who sees me sees him who sent me" (12:45). Surely it is not merely a matter of seeing a person of flesh and blood.

We have already noticed that "to come" and "to believe" are used synonymously. It is obvious in the parallelism between "to eat" and "to drink" (6:35), but food and drink in this gospel are not what one normally imagines. They serve to emphasize the dualism that characterizes the gospel. In this case, however, it is not a vertical dualism, but a horizontal one. Instead of contrasting the "above" to the "below" it contrasts "that which perishes" to "that which endures." To think that one lives to work for the food that perishes is to live deceived on the basis of false premises. On the contrary, in life one should work for the food "which endures to eternal life" (6:27). When the disciples who have left Jesus seated on the rim of Jacob's well return from the nearby town with food for Jesus' lunch, he explains to them that his food is not material. To eat is not to nourish the body; it is to hear, to obey. Jesus says to them: "My food is to do the will of him who sent me, and to accomplish his work" (4:34). This declaration is the premise of his farewell prayer (17:4) and of his words on the cross: "It is accomplished" [it is finished] (19:30). For humans to eat the food that endures to eternal life is to accomplish "their work." The work that they must accomplish is to believe in the One Sent by the Father (6:29). This work is "to eat" and "to drink." "He who eats my flesh and drinks my blood abides in me, and I in him" (6:56). In other words, to eat and to drink, "to believe," is to have the word of Jesus abiding in the believer (5:38).

With that, we have arrived at the central verb in the gospel *According to John*. The Greek verb is *menein*. Unfortunately most modern readers fail to realize its frequent use. In English (RSV) it is translated with seven different verbs which cover the semantic field of the Greek verb. *Menein* is translated "to be" as in "to be with you forever" (14:16); "to stay" as in "saw where he was staying" (1:39); "to remain" as in "it remained on him" (1:32); "to rest" as in "rests upon him" (3:36); "to continue" as in "the slave does not continue in the house forever" (8:35); "to endure" as in "endures to eternal life" (6:27), and "to abide" as in "unless it abides in the vine" (15:4). The core idea is "to dwell," "to be comfortable at home," "to have roots in time and space," "to abide." It is not by chance that the narration of Jesus' life begins with two disciples of John the Baptist who, having heard the testimony of John, decide to follow Jesus. Noticing that he is being followed, Jesus turns and asks them: "What do you seek?" They respond with another question: "Rabbi, where are you staying [abiding]?" (1:38). In effect, this is the question that the gospel invites all its readers to ask.

The answer to this question is decisive. The true disciple is the one who abides in the word of Jesus (8:31). Those who abide in Jesus and in whom the word of Jesus abides have direct access to God's will (15:7). Christians must be organically united, comfortable at home, rooted in space and time with Jesus, just as the branch is in the vine (15:4 – 6). To those who believe in him and in God, Jesus invites to the "abodes" [mansions] in the house of his Father (14:1 – 2). The gospel's promise is that the Father has many abodes for those who believe and abide in Jesus, that is, those in whom his word abides. This promise may be fulfilled immediately. Jesus says, "If a man loves me, he will keep my word, and my Father will love him, and we will come to him and make our home [abode] with him" (14:23). To the question, "Where do you abide?" Jesus' answered, "Come and see." The narrator then relates that they "came and saw where he was staying [abiding] and they stayed [abode] with him" (1:39).

To read *According to John* is an act of contemplation. It is an invitation to abide in the word of Jesus that insists on the oneness of the Father and the Son. Those who hear it come to him; those who are comfortable at home with Jesus and the Father endure (abide) to eternal life. As an invitation to abide in the company of Jesus, the emphasis placed on the need to come, to see, to eat, to drink, to believe is given its rationale. All these necessary steps are only means to an end. Eternal life is not an idealized theological concept to be grasped intellectually. It is a concrete reality to be grasped by life itself in its everyday experiences. That God is one is not established by negating the existence of other gods. It is fully understood only when it affirms the oneness of the Father, the Son, and all those in whom the Father and the Son abide. That is why the incarnation of the *Logos* is not only a new event in the life of God; it is also a new reality in the human beings who believe it.

This gospel uses simple language with strong philosophical connotations, but its theological framework does not communicate esoteric knowledge. Its purpose is not to provide a set of doctrines that teach what needs to be known by those who will live eternally. *According to John* makes the point that the possession of true doctrines is not the condition on which the Father grants eternal life. Rather the willingness to do the Father's will is the perquisite for the understanding of doctrines. It is the willingness to live by the commandment to love one another that enables the evaluation of doctrines. Jesus declares: "If any man's will is to do his will, he shall know whether the teaching [doctrine] is from God" (7:17). It is by abiding in his word that disciples become able to evaluate the soundness of doctrines. Thus, the gospel does not aim to bring about intellectual enlightenment. For those facing everyday life in the world below, it traces a way of life that conforms to the will of God and abides in the love of the Father and the Son. This is the "abode" prepared for the believers by the Father who loves them. This gospel is not interested in passing out saving information. Its aim is to be the *Logos* in which those who believe may abide. To hear, to come, to see, to eat, to drink, to believe, to keep his commandments is "to abide in my love" (15:9).

EPILOGUE

After their Lord had been seen alive on Sunday, the obvious problem for all the followers of Jesus was that he had been crucified on Friday. That had been a most embarrassing event. Crucifixion was the cruelest and most dishonorable way in which the death penalty could be administered. Christians, I am sure, would have given anything to have had Jesus die some other way. The truth was that he had been crucified on charges of sedition. When he was crucified all his disciples felt his mission had ended in shameful failure. While news that Jesus was alive and had been seen by some of his disciples gave them a new vision of the significance of Jesus' life, the fact that he had been crucified did not go away. That fact had to be integrated into an explanation of what they believed God had been doing through Jesus.

Christians explained the crucifixion in different ways. The author of *To the Hebrews* saw it as a sacrifice for the cleansing of the conscience. As such, it belonged to a different order than the sacrifices of heifers and rams offered for the infringement of purity laws prescribed in the Torah. Paul saw it within the framework provided by apocalyptic conceptions of the passing of the ages. It brought about the end of the present evil age ruled since the Fall by evil powers. The author of the letter *To the Colossians* saw it as the circumcision that makes perfect the cosmic body of which Christ is now the head. The gospel *According to Mark* sees it as the ransom payment that redeems humanity held captive by sin. *According to Luke* sees it as the supreme example of the noble death which in the Roman world was held as the ultimate achievement of a virtuous life.

According to John sees Jesus on the cross as the banner that gathers people who exercise faith in its symbolic function. Jesus had to be crucified. He could not die any other way. The one thing for which Moses is given credit is to have provided the central metaphor to the gospel. He lifted up a bronze serpent on a pole in the desert. Those bitten by highly venomous serpents were to look at the lifted up bronze serpent and live. According to the gospel, those dead in sins must believe in (look up to) Jesus lifted up on a cross and live. Only crucifixion would lift him up and make him the object of faith. Faith is not a strong feeling about something indefinable. It must have a discreet object in view.

The incarnation, the descent of the Son into the world of humanity, had as its only purpose to bring life to those who, while living, are dead in sin. The incarnate *Logos* lived among women and men on a course toward the "hour" when his mission would be accomplished. Human beings in the world of the flesh receive eternal life when they are confronted with the crucified and believe that he is the One Sent by the Father. *According to John* does not teach resignation, patient endurance, obedience to the law of Moses, the need for repentance, or the need to be crucified with Christ. It teaches that God glorified the Son when the Son was lifted up on a cross, and that those who believe in him receive eternal life. In other words, the highly embarrassing, disqualifying, humiliating crucifixion is the place where faith in the incarnation is tested. The crucifixion is the ascent, the return trip of the Son back to the Father. It is where the unity of the Father and the Son is demonstrated and the glory of the love that unites them is revealed. How the *Logos* became incarnate, when, how, where, to whom was he born, is passed over in silence. What is emphasized is *that* he *descended* from heaven and dwelt "in the flesh." *How* he *ascended* is described in some detail. He was crucified at Golgotha, outside Jerusalem, by Roman soldiers on orders from Pilate the Roman procurator.

During his life he did some amazing things that functioned as signs. They pointed to the work he had come to accomplish. Their role as signs, however, could not be recognized before what they pointed to became available. In other words, it was only after the crucifixion that the disciples understood his life as a giving of signs directing attention to the cross. It has often been said that Christianity without the cross is like the world without the sun. That is certainly the point made by *According to John*. It is at the cross that the life and light, the two primary properties of the *Logos*, become available to all those who look at it with faith. In the language of the gospel, the cross is where the Son of man is glorified.

As said in the first sentence of the Introduction, the cross is the most certain of all historical events in the life of Jesus. Its significance for Christians, however, totally transcends its historicity. As this gospel says, it is the Sign to which all signs point. It is the visual object on which faith in the incarnation is demonstrated. As Paul Tillich liked to insist, the cross is the most perfect of all symbols because, even though its historical facticity is beyond doubt, reducing its meaning to its historicity is to emphasize an execution and miss the point. Its shamefulness as a historical event, however, prevents it from ever becoming an idol. Those who worship the crucified cannot fail to see the cross as only the Sign of the triumph of the divine life over eschatological death. Only those who see Jesus crucified as the One Sent by the Father worship him — as the man born blind after his sight was restored did.

In this symbolic universe, where shame and glory are one, the signs and their object are one. Here the Father and the Son are one, and the flesh and the Spirit can become one in the incarnate *Logos*. That is the crux of the gospel *According to John*. Those who live in the world below, in the flesh, can have eternal life in the Spirit. They can transcend the apparently unbridgeable chasm that separates the human from the divine world and abide in the Father and the Son. Rather than proposing that Christians live escaping from their condition in the world to an otherworldly spiritual realm, the gospel affirms the necessity to live fully incarnated in the world to which Christians are sent as agents of peace and life. As those born of water and the Spirit they impersonate the union of the material and the spiritual.

The community of those born from above is the present manifestation of the persistent love of God for the world. The universe has been united and is sustained by the love that has united the

Father and the Son since before the foundation of the world. The existence of such a community in the world, one which is not glued together by force, ideology, ecclesiastical structures or authority but by love, is a testimony to the truth that the Father and the Son have been glorified at the cross. The love that unites the disciples who live by the Spirit is the most powerful witness to the truth of the Gospel.

This magnificent vision of the significance of the incarnation and its final glorification on earth by a beloved closely-knit community of disciples who abide in the love of the Father and the Son is both a blessed ideal and a dangerous trap. Those who believe in the Son as the One Sent by the Father do not desire any thing more than to live abiding in the midst of lovers who reveal themselves in the glory of the cross. But the sense of being part of a select, chosen few with a special mission to the world can be the most powerful temptation to sectarian aloofness and spiritual pride. *According to John* boldly opens the way for mortals to have eternal life and also tempts them to look at themselves as better than the rest of humanity, that other outside "world." Admiration for the magnificent theological vision of the significance and function of the crucifixion must not prevent awareness of the blind spot in its underside. It may not have been a factor to the Christians who lived in the troubling circumstances of their emergence *vis a vis* Rabbinic Judaism and an array of different Christianities. It is a dangerous blind spot which can undo the ability of Christians to witness to the love of God in the globalized world of the twenty first century.

Claiming to take seriously *According to John,* Christians at times conceive themselves as apart from "the world" and think it is a matter of either/or. To the contrary, the gospel affirms the both/and of the Father and the Son, of the Spirit and the flesh, and of "in the world" and "in the Spirit." The power of the love of God gives life to those who live in the world below. Thus, Spirit and flesh are one not only in the incarnate Logos but also in the believers. It is tragic when those who see themselves as the beneficiaries of God's uniting love insist on a non-incarnational, sectarian either/

or: either life in the Spirit or life in the world. The *Gospel* of the gospel *According to John* is that God's effective love brings peace to those who believe, and peace is the fruit of both/and. Thus the challenge of this gospel is for the beneficiaries of this peace not to become cocooned in a separate world, but to embrace the world below with the love of the Father who sent the incarnate Son on a mission to extend the power of life and freedom.

The truth that makes people free is not an esoteric piece of knowledge to be hoarded and protected, or proclaimed with elitist self-satisfaction. It is a source of life that is to be shared with joy. The gospel's polemic against trips to heaven and the possession of private information aims to deny the effectiveness of such claims to exclusivity. As Jesus tells Pilate, all his activity was done in public squares, the synagogues and the temple. He did nothing in secret. At the core of this gospel is this openness, this prodigal giving of the Spirit that engenders abundant life to the world. This openness enables believers, as grateful recipients of the freedom of the truth that extend to the world the grace upon grace with which they have been blessed, to be full participants in the world below.

According to John is an amazing document. From a purely literary point of view, it is an impressive achievement, considering the way its dialogues are constructed, arguments are developed, dramas are built, irony keeps things out of balance, and double meanings play tricks on its protagonists and its readers. All these testify to a very literate community of Christians who were quite removed from village artisans, peasants from the countryside or fishermen from the Sea of Galilee. In fact, the gospel reflects a sophisticated theological position arrived at after much reflection and some anguish.

The literary qualities of the text are fully matched, and even surpassed, by the profound theological vision it gives to those confused by the distractions and the tribulations encountered by all women and men living in the world below. That vision is nothing less than a new understanding of the divine reality, an understanding that challenges all to live free in the Spirit by the power of love – the love that causes lovers to identify themselves in those being loved.

Index of References to *According to John*

1:1 .... 18, 47	1:41 119
1:3 .... 19, 46, 54	1:45 .... 60, 95, 164
1:4 .... 109, 184	1:46 200
1:4 – 5 29	1:47 .... 52, 126
1:9 51	1:49 60
1:10 .... 101, 103	1:51 .... 52, 67
1:12 – 13 42	
1:13 .... 164, 174	2:1 81
1:14 .... 38, 47, 48, 109, 206	2:1 – 11 9
1:15 26	2:4, 6 82
1:15 – 20 15	2:4, 23 192
1:16 .... 47, 48	2:6 189
1:17 .... 28, 54, 93, 98	2:6 – 11 15
1:18 .... 23, 29, 45, 48, 56	2:11 136
1:20 .... 26, 62, 119	2:7 82
1:21 – 22 26	2:10 83
1:29 110	2:11 .... 83, 88
1:29 – 34 3	2:13 77
1:31 152	2:13 – 22 86
1:32 – 33 .... 110, 144, 208	2:21 ...... 43, 49, 73, 107, 192
1:34 .... 26, 207	2:22 88
1:38 208	2:23 – 25 88
1:39 .... 208, 209	2:24 – 25 3

3:1 6
3:2 .... 79, 89, 164
3:3 .... 54, 110, 153
3:5 .... 41, 78, 153, 188
3:6 .... 38, 111, 153, 155
3:8 ....54, 70
3:9 89
3:10 152
3:11 5
3:12 110
3:13 .... 113, 202
3:13 .... 37, 66
3:14 – 15 40
3:15, 16, 36 ....
 .... 165, 171, 192, 208
3:16 .... 40, 97
3:16 – 17 .... 102, 171, 184
3:17 103
3:19 33
3:21 55
3:22 151
3:25 153
3:26 .... 24, 152
3:28 .... 62, 119
3:31 – 32 .... 54, 55
3:33 67
3:34 .... 54, 80, 115, 157
3:36 103

4:1 .... 151, 188
4:2 .... 26, 152, 188
4:6 164
4:10 191
4:10, 14 55

4:13 – 15 189
4:14 78
4:19, 26, 29, 42 62
4:21 176
4:22 127
4:23 .... 74, 113, 127
4:24 .... 49, 55, 56, 115
4:25 – 26 119
4:34 208
4:34 – 36 .... 71, 91
4:40 178
4:42 .... 94, 119, 145
4:44 69
4:46 – 54 .... 9, 159
4:52 165
4:53 88

5:1 – 16 159
5:16, 18 .... 127, 163, 175
5:17 .... 25, 64, 162
5:18 .... 23, 64
5:19 26
5:19 – 30 .... 163, 164
5:20 90
5:21 26
5:21 – 30 90
5:22 25
5:22 – 24 103
5:25, 28 74
5:26 26
5:27 .... 25, 67
5:30 26
5:31 26
5:36 26
5:37 – 38 27

5:38 208	7:2 77
5:39 .... 94, 206	7:4 101
5:41 127	7:5, 30 71
5:42 – 44 27	7:6 71
5:45 – 46 94	7:6, 8 .... 191, 192
	7:12 – 14 191
6:2 – 4 89	7:15 – 24 10
6:4 77	7:17 .... 54, 210
6:8 137	7:18 53
6:15 .... 61, 89, 197	7:19 94
6:16 – 21 106	7:19 – 23 .... 160 – 161
6:20 .... 107, 190	7:20, 27 130
6:26 89	7:28 53
6:27 .... 207, 208	7:31 127
6:27, 49, 53 .... 51, 66	7:31, 35 60
6:32 .... 52, 97	7:37 – 39 .... 78, 191
6:33 55	7:39 .... 120, 193
6:35 .... 154, 206, 207	7:41 – 42 .... 63, 198
6:39, 40, 44, 54 37	7:44 30
6:40, 47, 54 165	7:48 130
6:42 .... 38, 60	7:50 .... 6, 79, 147, 164
6:51 .... 103, 154	7:51 127
6:52 60	
6:53 – 56 52	8:11 146
6:56 – 57 .... 154, 207	8:12 .... 30, 55
6:60 .... 119, 136, 155	8:13 130
6:62 .... 38, 66	8:14 53
6:63 ... 52, 78, 91, 111, 155, 158	8:16 53
6:64 89	8:17 93
6:66 137	8:20 .... 30, 71
6:68 158	8:21 – 24 38
6:69 .... 119, 137	8:23 .... 39, 60, 104, 198
6:70 – 71 135	8:25 .... 38, 120
	8:27 – 29 120
7:1, 25, 30 127	8:28 .... 39, 66, 113

8:31......52, 55, 127, 158, 208	10:17..................................172
8:32, 36...............................184	10:18......................................3
8:35 – 36........................55, 208	10:22 – 23..........................80
8:40, 59...............................127	10:24............................62,119
8:41 – 44................................53	10:25....................................90
8:43......................................206	10:26....................................63
8:45..53	10:27..................................206
8:51...................97, 114, 158	10:28 – 29..........................90
8:59.......................................30	10:30............23, 64, 81, 175
	10:31....................30, 81, 127
9:1 – 14.............................159	10:33..................................175
9:2..11	10:32 – 33.....................64, 90
9:4.......................................164	10: 34..................84, 93, 127
9:12..32	10:35....................................65
9:15.....................................164	10:36.....................64, 95, 157
922...21	10:38............23, 64, 90, 175
9:22, 34..............................129	10:39....................................30
9:24..............................23, 32	
9:25..32	11:2............................ 140, 147
9:28.....................................127	11:3................... 140, 169, 178
9:29.............32, 95, 127, 200	11:4......... 138, 169, 179, 183
9:31..95	11:5.................. 148, 169, 173
9:32..32	11:7.. 138
9:34..21	11:9 – 10.............33, 79, 102
9:35 – 37.......................66, 67	11:11.........................104, 179
9:37...........................119, 127	11:15 – 16................138, 179
9:38.................................3, 32	11:24....................................37
9:39...................67, 103, 207	11:25.........................146, 180
9:41.....................................127	11:25 – 26........................184
	11:25, 27......................63, 73,
10:1 – 18...........................125	11:27........101, 119, 146, 180
10:4..................... 60, 97, 174	11:28..................................181
10:6..................... 30, 120, 171	11:33..................................181
10:10..........54, 107, 112, 127	11:34..................................146
10:15 – 16...........................171	11:35 – 36................169, 182

11:37 – 38 182	12:35 33
11:40 183	12:36 .... 30, 164
11:41 183	12:37 89
11:42 200	12:42 129
11:44 183	12:42 – 43 6
11:45 127	12:45 207
11:45 – 46 .... 184, 206	12:46 33
11:47 89	12:47 103
11:48 70	12:50 .... 97, 113
11:50 – 52 .... 172, 175, 200	
11:53 .... 61, 128, 184	13:1 .... 71, 155
11:55 .... 77, 153	13:1, 3 79
11:57 30	13:2 .... 104, 156
	13:6 – 7 .... 120, 137
12:1 – 2 172	13:8 – 10 156
12:1, 9 – 10 140	13:10 – 17 10
12:3 .... 147, 173	13:13 – 15 .... 156, 174
12:9 – 10 89	13:16 157
12:10 .... 128, 178	13:17 156
12:11, 42 127	13:26 140
12:12 – 19 61	13:27 .... 72, 104
12:16 120	13:30 .... 79, 164
12:18 89	13:31 66
12:19 101	13:34 .... 97, 169
12:20 – 21 98	13:36 – 37 137
12;21 207	
12:21, 23 .... 39, 66, 71 73	14:1 .... 113, 209
12:23 .... 137, 156, 207	14:3 .... 47, 114
12:24 .... 70, 148	14:6 54
12:25 .... 105, 168	14:9 .... 23, 64
12:27 207	14:12 .... 91, 107, 165
12:28 114	14:16 – 17 .... 103, 110, 208
12:31 .... 103, 104, 114	14:17 .... 55, 113
12:32 .... 39, 197, 202	14:18 113
12:34 .... 39, 63, 66, 67	14:21 .... 174, 175, 176

14:22 138	16:27, 30 200
14:23 .... 97, 176, 209	16:28 .... 40, 104
14:25 122	16:29 – 30 120
14:26 .... 122, 126	16:32 74
14:27 .... 107, 115	16:33 .... 104, 105, 107, 115
14:30 104	
14:31 .... 10, 170	17:1 90
14:33 135	17:3 .... 63, 200
	17:4 .... 90, 107, 208
15:3, 7 158	17:5 .... 71, 101
15:4 .... 208, 209	17:8 87
15:7 208	17:14 97
15:9 .... 176, 210	17:14 – 17 98
15:10 .... 84, 170	15:15 104
15:12 97	17:17 .... 98, 157
15:15 158	17:18 105
15:17 .... 10, 169	17:21 – 22 .... 24, 102
15:18 103	17:24 .... 71, 101, 170
15:19 104	17:25 103
15:20 124	17:26 175
15:23 – 24 168	
15:24 90	18:1 10
15:25 .... 90, 127	18:1 – 8 30
15:26 .... 55, 113	18:6 196
	18:10 137
16:2 .... 21, 129	18:17, 29, 30 60
16:2, 4 72	18:19 196
16:4 122	18:20 .... 101, 119
16:7 113	18:28 154
16:8 – 9 114	18:29 – 30 197
16:11 .... 104, 114	18:31 .... 84, 93, 127
16:13 .... 55, 114	18:32 197
16:14 115	18:33 197
16:18 30	18:35 – 36 198
16:21 .... 11, 72	18:37 .... 102, 198, 206

18:37 – 38..........55	21:2, 7..........140
18:38..........199	21:2 – 13..........139
	21:11..........139
19:4, 6..........199	21;15 – 19..........139
19:5..........200	21:23..........139
19:7....... 60, 84, 95, 127, 199	21:24 – 25..........10
19:9.......... 38,199	
19:10 – 11..........39	
19:11..........3, 73	
19:12, 21..........60	
19:14, 15, 19..........61	
19:19..........201	
19:20 – 22..........202	
19:26 – 27..........149	
19:30....71, 91, 106, 196, 208	
19:31..........80	
19:34..........78, 201	
19:35..........202	
19:38..........129, 172	
19:38 – 39..........6, 22, 79	
19:39..........147, 164	
19:40..........80, 153	
20:8.......... 3	
20:9.......... 120, 148	
29:17 – 18..........148, 158	
20:18..........97	
20:19..........22, 115, 129, 148	
20:21..........105	
20:22..........12, 74, 115	
20:28..........24, 138	
20:30 – 31..........9, 10, 27, 88	
20:31..........165	
21:2.......... 139	

ALSO BY HEROLD WEISS
FROM ENERGION PUBLICATIONS

For those who believe that one can be both scholarly and faithful, this is a 'must read' book!
Dr. Robert R. LaRochelle
UCC Pastor and author of
Crossing the Street

Reading Weiss was a prophetic touch to my own life.
Joel Watts
Unsettled Christianity
(unsettledchristianity.com)

MORE FROM ENERGION PUBLICATIONS

Personal Study
Finding My Way in Christianity	Herold Weiss	$16.99
Holy Smoke! Unholy Fire	Bob McKibben	$14.99
The Jesus Paradigm	David Alan Black	$17.99
When People Speak for God	Henry Neufeld	$17.99
The Sacred Journey	Chris Surber	$11.99

Christian Living
Faith in the Public Square	Robert D. Cornwall	$16.99
Grief: Finding the Candle of Light	Jody Neufeld	$8.99
My Life Story	Becky Lynn Black	$14.99
Crossing the Street	Robert LaRochelle	$16.99
Life as Pilgrimage	David Moffett-Moore	14.99

Bible Study
Learning and Living Scripture	Lentz/Neufeld	$12.99
From Inspiration to Understanding	Edward W. H. Vick	$24.99
Philippians: A Participatory Study Guide	Bruce Epperly	$9.99
Ephesians: A Participatory Study Guide	Robert D. Cornwall	$9.99

Theology
Creation in Scripture	Herold Weiss	$12.99
Creation: the Christian Doctrine	Edward W. H. Vick	$12.99
The Politics of Witness	Allan R. Bevere	$9.99
Ultimate Allegiance	Robert D. Cornwall	$9.99
History and Christian Faith	Edward W. H. Vick	$9.99
The Journey to the Undiscovered Country	William Powell Tuck	$9.99
Process Theology	Bruce G. Epperly	$4.99

Ministry
Clergy Table Talk	Kent Ira Groff	$9.99
Out of This World	Darren McClellan	$24.99

Generous Quantity Discounts Available
Dealer Inquiries Welcome
Energion Publications — P.O. Box 841
Gonzalez, FL 32560
Website: http://energionpubs.com
Phone: (850) 525-3916

www.ingramcontent.com/pod-product-compliance
Lightning Source LLC
LaVergne TN
LVHW090115080426
835507LV00040B/854